PAST & PRESENT

WILLIAMSPORT

Opposite: The Philadelphia & Reading passenger station was located at the foot of Pine Street. In this c. 1900 photograph, it can be seen beside the gable-roofed freight station on the left with the engineer's office behind it on the right. In the background on the right is the Market Street Bridge. Today, much of this location is the site of an interstate highway. (Courtesy of Pete DiBartolomeo.)

Past & Present

WILLIAMSPORT

Elaine M. Decker

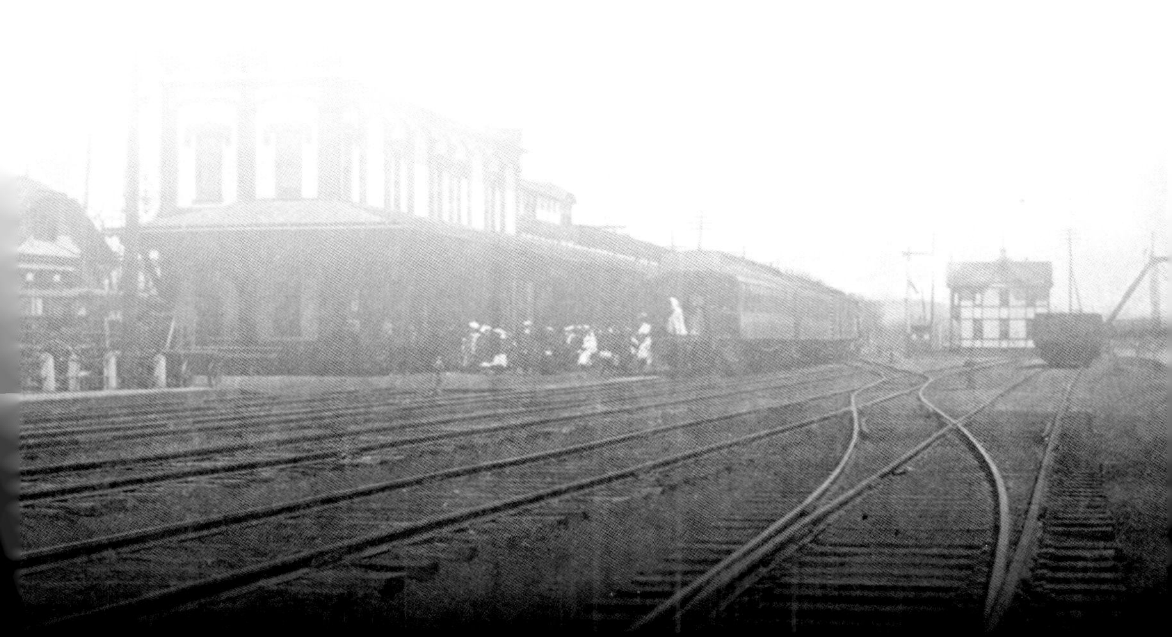

ISBN 978-1-4671-0284-1

Library of Congress Control Number: 2018951129

Published by Arcadia Publishing
Charleston, South Carolina

Printed in the United States of America

For all general information, please contact Arcadia Publishing:
Telephone 843-853-2070
Fax 843-853-0044
E-mail sales@arcadiapublishing.com
For customer service and orders:
Toll-Free 1-888-313-2665

Visit us on the Internet at www.arcadiapublishing.com

On the Front Cover: Third and Market Streets were widened where they intersect to accommodate market stalls, wagons, and shoppers and form Market Square. Permanent storefronts surrounded the square. Today, the buildings are still set back, but the street is no longer wider at the intersection. A baseball diamond with life-sized bronze statues has been placed here to celebrate the history of Little League and Carl Stotz, its founder. Williamsport is the birthplace of Little League Baseball and home to the Little League World Series. (Then, courtesy of Pete DiBartolomeo; now, photograph by the author.)

On the Back Cover: The Williamsport High School building, seen in the background, saw its first graduating class in 1914, though the building was incomplete at the time. A fire had damaged the previous school building, forcing students into their new place before it was finished. The school shown here ceased being a high school when a new one was built farther west in the city, opening in 1972. Today, this old high school is the George S. Klump Academic Center, part of the Pennsylvania College of Technology campus. (Courtesy of Pete DiBartolomeo.)

Contents

ACKNOWLEDGMENTS

This book could not have been written without the help of many people and their mutual interest in the history of Williamsport. First, I would like to thank Pete DiBartolomeo, who provided every vintage photograph and postcard in this book. His generosity in sharing this amazing collection of historical memorabilia is why this book has happened.

So many people have assisted me in my research and provided inspiration that it would be impossible to name everyone who influenced this project, but that doesn't lessen how appreciative I am. You know who you are, and I sincerely thank you.

There are a few people, however, who I feel I need to mention specifically, and I am so grateful for their contributions. In no particular order, huge thanks go out to Park Place, the City of Williamsport, Luke Hinshaw and Joseph Trepanowski, the staff of the Cell Block, the staff and residents at the Williamsport Home and "C" Building, Bruce Huffman, Mary Sieminski, the Williamsport Scottish Rite, First Church United Methodist, the Thomas T. Taber Museum, and Dana Brigandi, Toby Schwartzman, and all the helpful staff at the James V. Brown Library.

I want to thank Jimmie the Owl (whose story is in this book) for reminding me to follow my instincts, even if it means sitting still until you figure it all out.

A warm thank-you particularly goes out to Stella. Her humor and support were constant reminders that this book was more than just a pipe dream.

I especially want to thank my family and my dear friend Joe who understood when I disappeared into the 19th century for hours and days at a time. They encouraged me, assisted me in taking every "present" photograph in this book, and helped me in many other numerous and significant ways—too many to list.

Finally, I would like to thank Arcadia Publishing for publishing this book, which has become a part of me.

Introduction

Many books have been written about Williamsport that offer a comprehensive history of the city. This is not one of them. Instead, this book takes the reader on a journey through moments in time, moments that were captured in photographs and postcards many years ago. There was a story when those photographs were taken, and there is a story now—sometimes more than one. Some of the stories were pivotal in the formation of Williamsport, but many of the narratives found in this book are descriptions of the everyday life of an average Williamsport citizen. Combined, these accounts are what made Williamsport what it is today. It is natural, therefore, to include a current photograph with the vintage image of each location, side by side, past and present. As if watching time go by, one can clearly see what changes Williamsport has seen and what has stayed the same.

Williamsport is located along the West Branch of the Susquehanna River. It is not a port as its name suggests and never was one, at least not in the traditional sense, but the river played a key role in the lumber boom of the 19th century. This lumber boom made millionaires of a select group of Williamsport citizens, and those millionaires built mansions and businesses and contributed greatly to the construction of many churches and organizations and to early Williamsport in general. The architecture and woodwork inside and outside many of the buildings are still breathtaking today. The mansions of the era can be seen all over Williamsport, including a section of West Fourth Street named Millionaire's Row. The "original millionaire's row" was east of Market Street; a few mansions survive there today. In addition, much of Grampian Boulevard is known for its huge homes, and mansions dot many other streets in the city. However, the majority of people lived in more modest homes. Some of those homes were luxurious, but compared to Williamsport's grander ones, these relatively simpler homes appear dwarfed in size and style. Alongside these impressive homes were also average neighborhoods where most people lived, and they also played a large role in the shaping of Williamsport. Not much has changed today. Some of the neighborhoods have been turned into student housing, and others have been removed to make way for expansion, but many remain just as they were a hundred years ago. A sample of these residential areas can be found in this book, which shows what they looked like at one time and what they look like now, along with some stories of the people and events that took place in them. Business districts, public spaces, and churches are also represented in these pages. Taken all together, the reader is invited to experience a sense of Williamsport as it once was and compare that era to what has developed over time.

Besides the prosperous lumber boom and the more recent natural-gas boom, both of which brought wealth to the area like few cities have ever seen, Williamsport has experienced its share of disaster. Several devastating fires, some taking entire city blocks, took their toll, but it was the floods that most drastically transformed the landscape. The major floods took many buildings, creating the need for those buildings to be reconstructed, renovated, or abandoned. With each flood, small and large, the city changed. Finally, the necessity for a levee system to protect the city was realized, and it transformed Williamsport once again, as the banks of the river were filled in and buildings removed to make way for the earthen wall. After the high embankments were completed, for the first time, the citizens of Williamsport could no longer see the river from the city. It must have been very odd for the citizens at the time to be visually cut off from something that had such a great impact on their lives. Today, the people of Williamsport are once again connected to the river from a view on the very popular Susquehanna Riverwalk, a path that follows the shore of the river atop the levee.

A new highway and new parks, a new college and an expansion of an existing college, the introduction of new industry and businesses, the renovation of government offices; all of these things transformed Williamsport through the years. But perhaps it is not the changes that are so extraordinary as what hasn't changed. Looking at the photographs of past and present, it quickly becomes apparent that much of the architecture has been preserved. Williamsport citizens love their history, and it shows. Homes, businesses, and many public buildings remain much as they were at the turn of the 20th century.

Today, the city is still growing and changing. New buildings and expansion are a common sight. Streets are being realigned to accommodate that growth, and entire sections of the city are being renovated. The collection of scenes in this book stop time for just an instant, allowing the reader to see the city from the past and again at the time when this book was written. It will be very interesting, therefore, to revisit these sets of images in a few years and a few decades because Williamsport is always changing, as any healthy, vibrant city does. Williamsport citizens respect and admire the past, enjoy the present, and look forward to what the future may bring. So, let's begin our journey now, join these citizens of Williamsport from different centuries, and see what they did and saw and are experiencing now.

CHAPTER 1

STREET SCENES

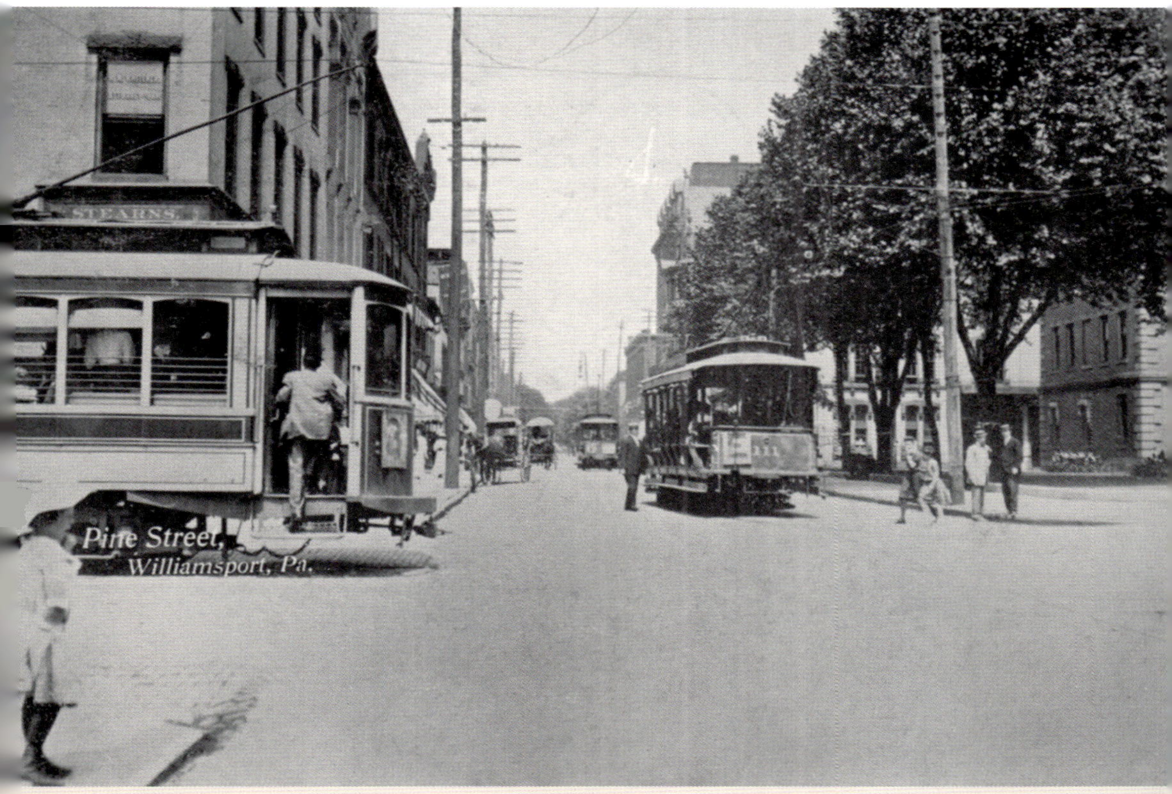

This view looking north on Pine Street is from the heyday of trolleys. The first trolley was placed on its line in 1854 and was horse-drawn. In 1891, as the head of the Williamsport Passenger Railway Company, Hiram R. Rhoads introduced the electrified trolley to Williamsport. Buses replaced trolleys in 1933 to reduce traffic congestion and provide faster travel.

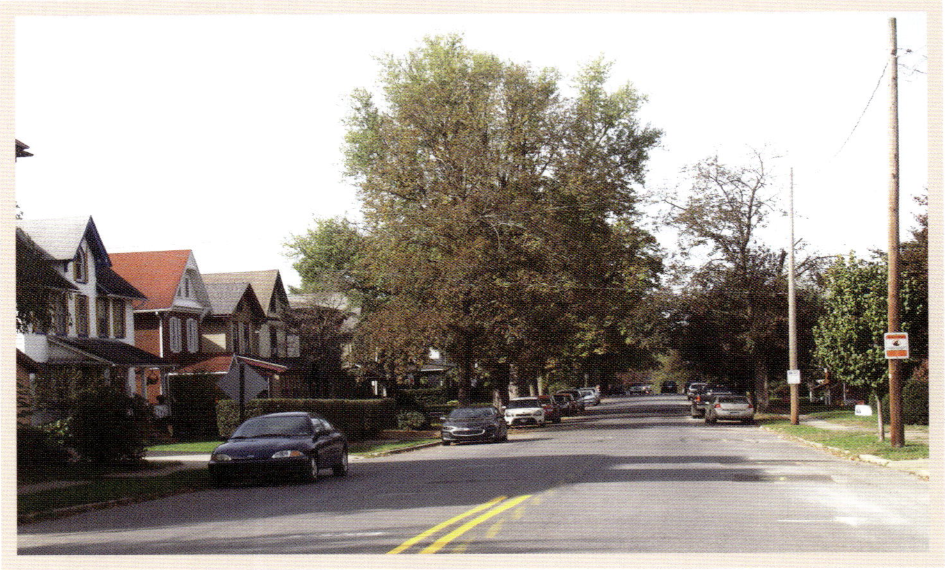

Rural Avenue, shown below around the turn of the 20th century, is one of several streets that converge at "Confusion Corner." The view is from the center of the intersection, facing west. Safety has always been a concern here. In 1960, when one of those converging streets was a state highway, the installation of a traffic circle was proposed. It never happened though, and today, stop signs on some, though not all, of the intersecting streets help cautious drivers navigate through.

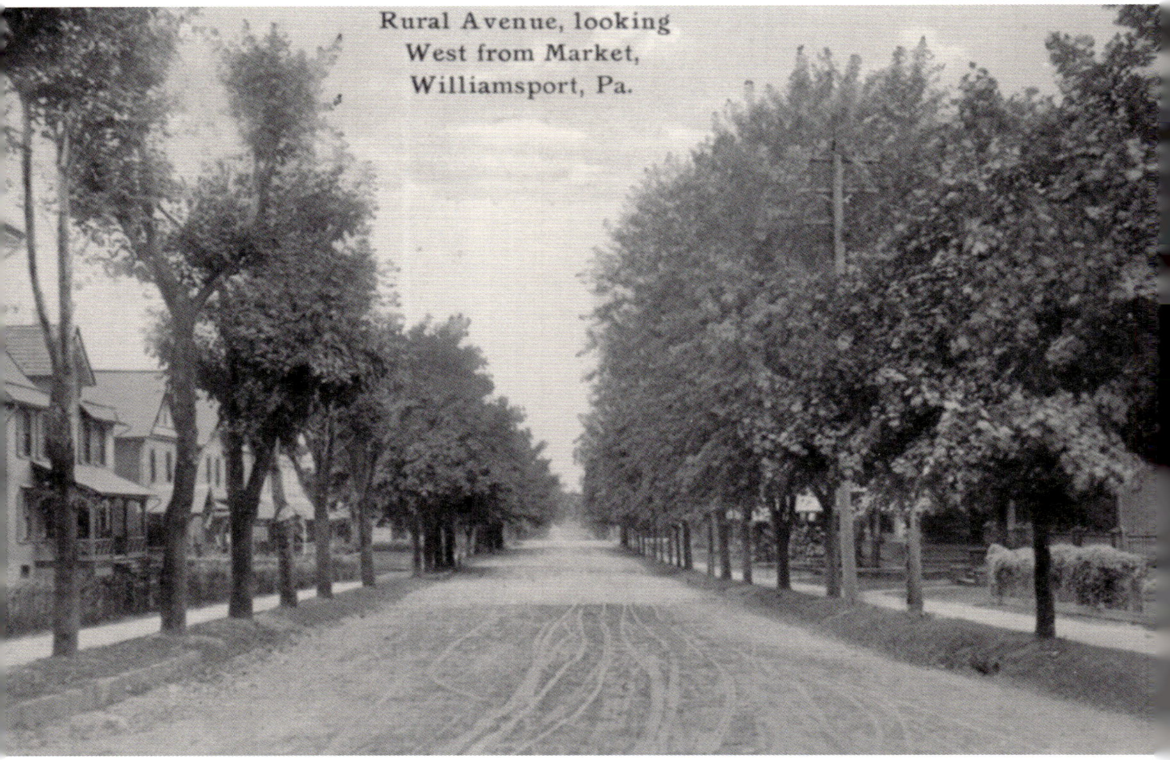

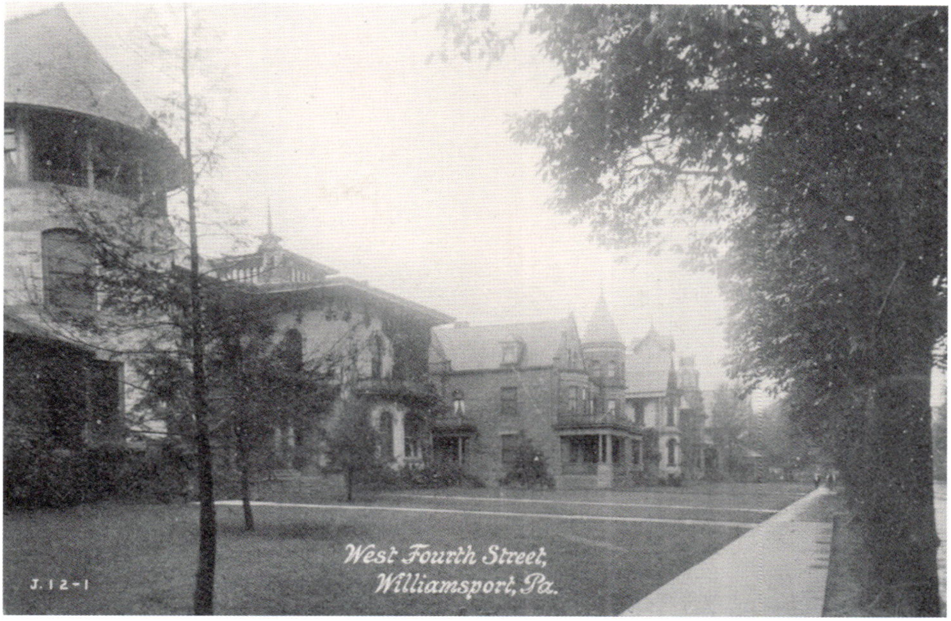

It is reputed that at one time Williamsport had more millionaires per capita than anywhere else in the United States. The intersection of Elmira and West Fourth Streets, looking west, marks the entrance to Millionaire's Row, where lumber barons from the mid- to late 1800s until the early 1900s built their mansions. Today, this section is being preserved and restored by many individuals and organizations, most notably Preservation Williamsport.

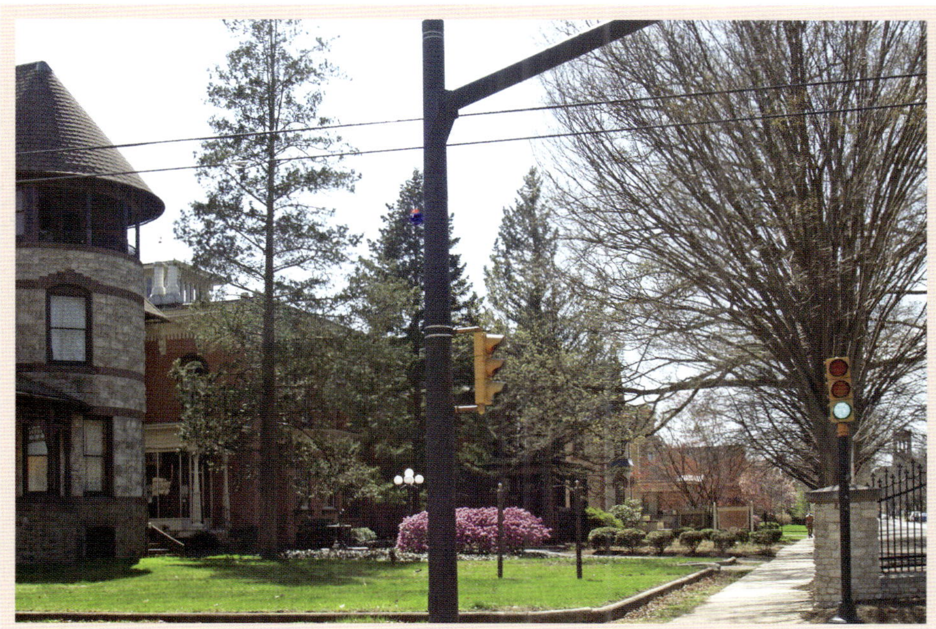

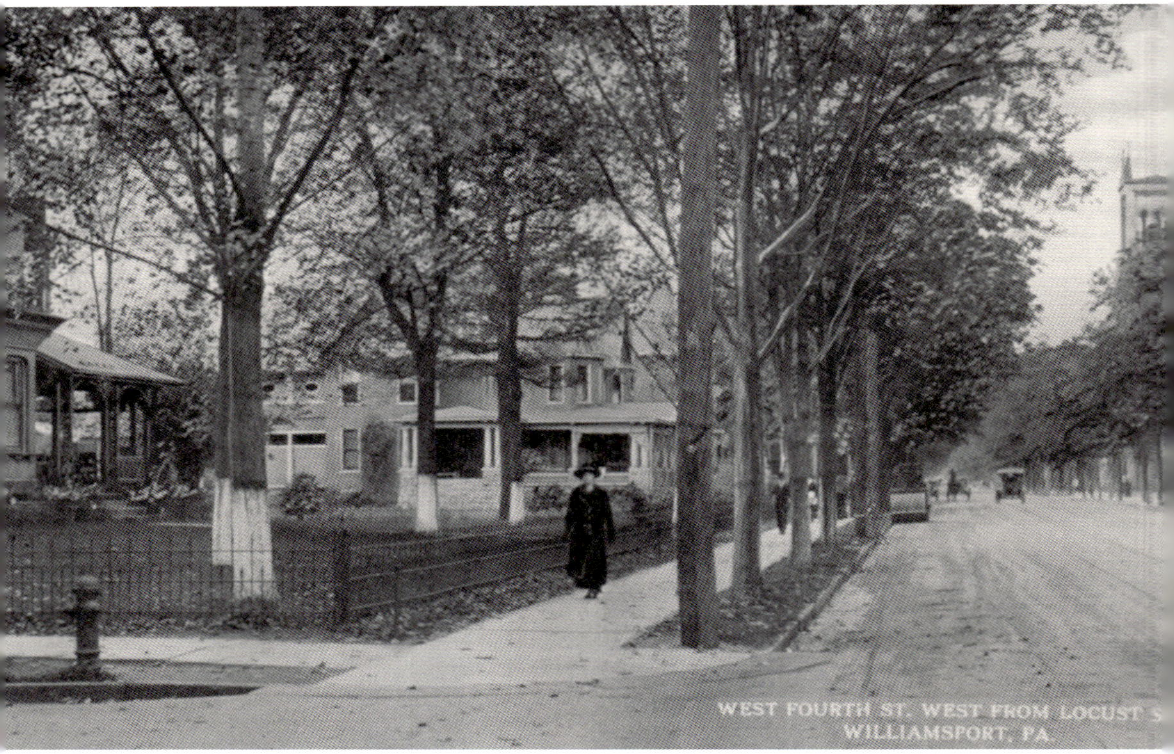

The home on the corner of Locust and West Fourth Streets is no longer there, but the house next to it, as seen in the center, is still standing. J. Walton Bowman had this home built in 1894. Bowman was a well-known and wealthy businessman for whom Bowman Field was named in recognition of his fundraising efforts and his own financial contribution to build the ballpark, which is today the second oldest minor-league park operating in the United States.

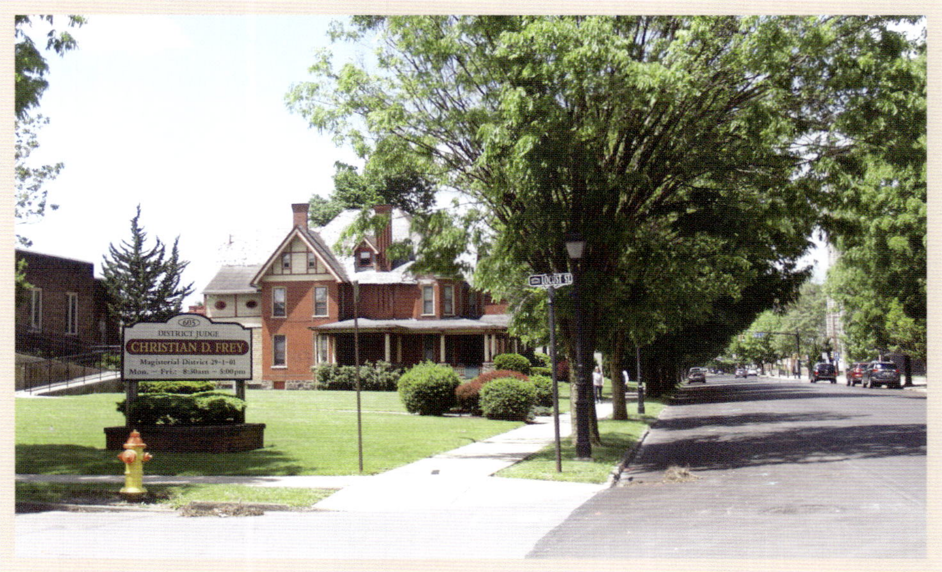

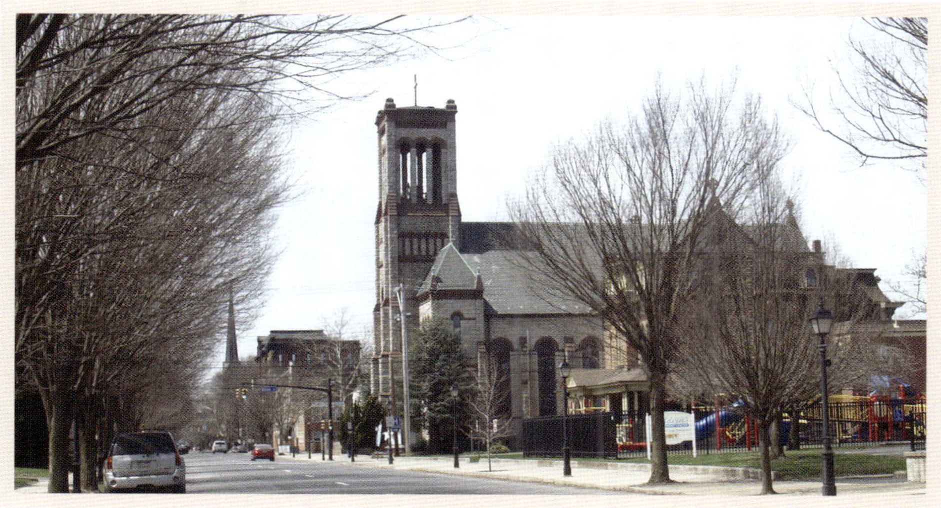

Looking west on West Fourth, the Church of the Annunciation was built here around 1889. The existing house east of the church was built in the 1860s for Henry B. Smith. Adjacent, the Kinyon residence, which is no longer there, made the news in December 1874. Loren C. Kinyon's hitched horse escaped for a speedy run through the city, startling drivers and pedestrians. Though runaway horses were common, this one traveled quite far before returning home safely.

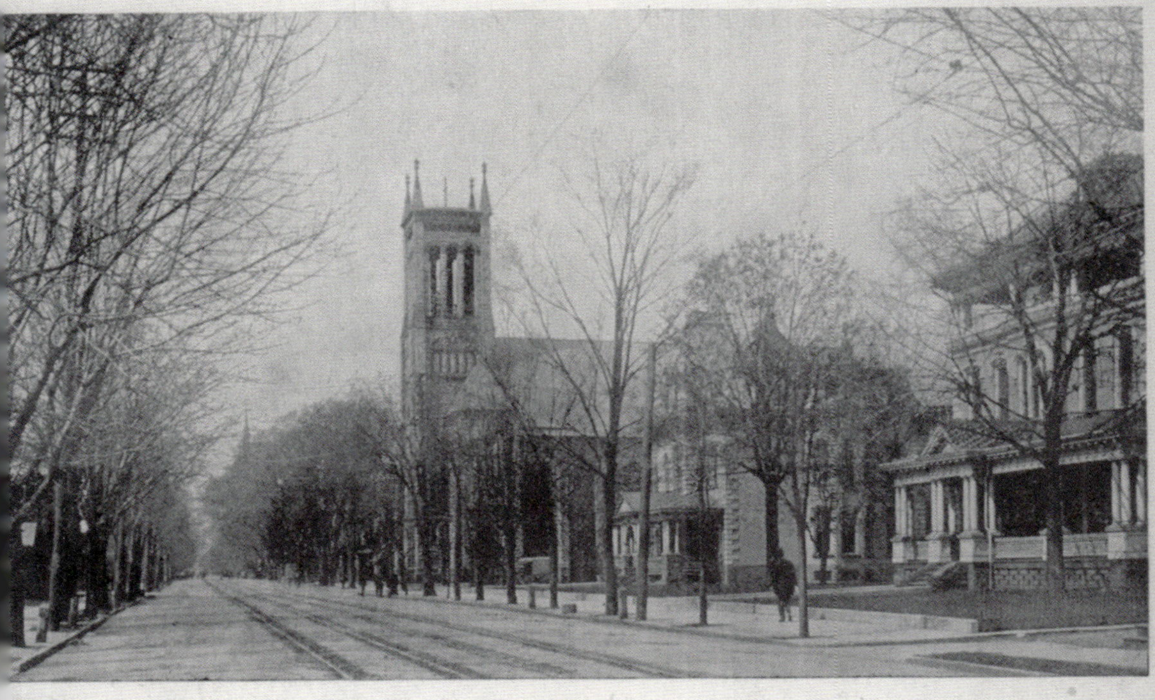

Fourth Street, West from Locust, Church of Annunciation, Williamsport, Pa

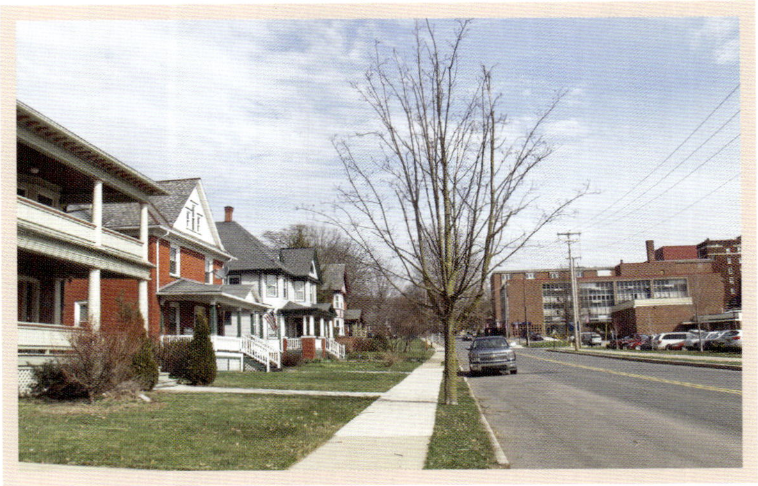

Not much has changed in this view of the west side of Campbell Street looking north. These houses were built in the early 1900s. They were owned by families whose income came from managing the typical industries of the time: lumber companies, planing mills, and coal and feed suppliers. One resident was an air brake inspector for the railroad. The east side, however, has seen great changes. Instead of homes, it is now a parking lot for University of Pittsburgh Medical Center (UPMC) Susquehanna.

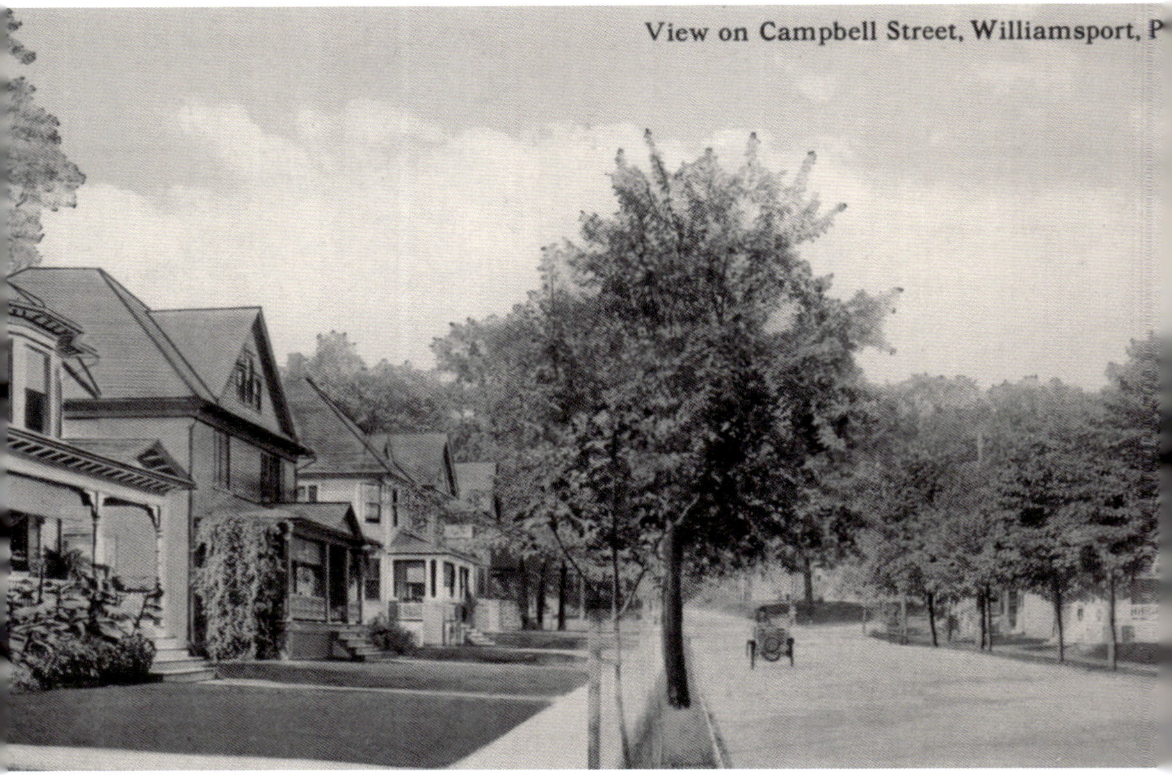

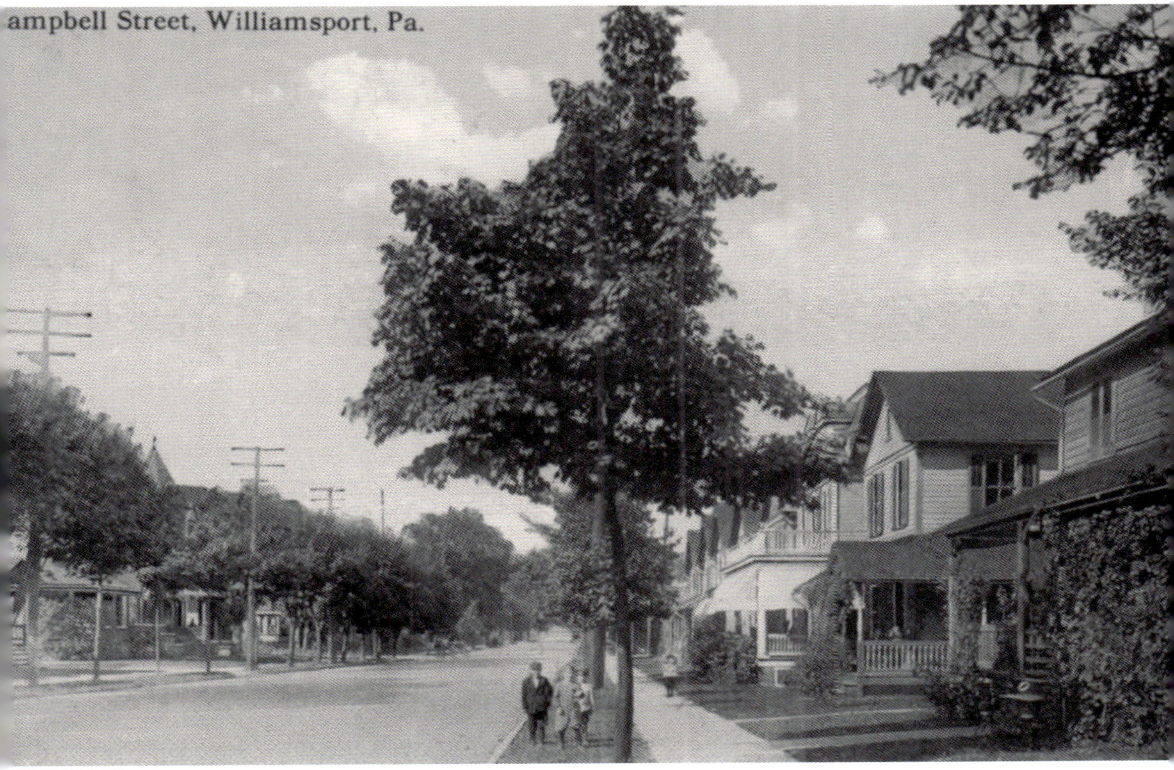

A representation of an average American residential street in the 1900s, on July 23, 1914, this block of Campbell Street made front-page news. A large crowd gathered here when a rehabilitated owl that had been returned to the wild decided to perch on an electric line. Several attempts were made to encourage Jimmie the Owl to leave for the mountains, but to no avail. The last report stated that he had not yet left.

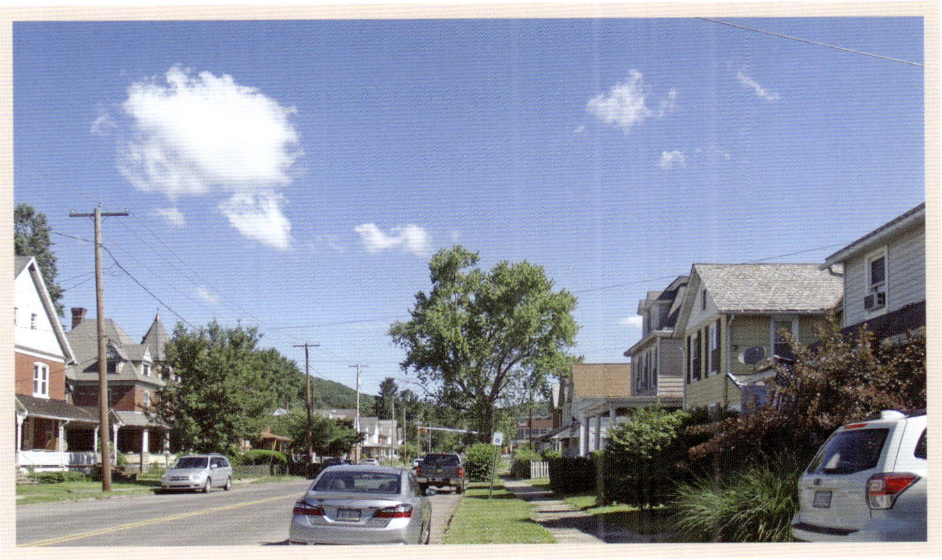

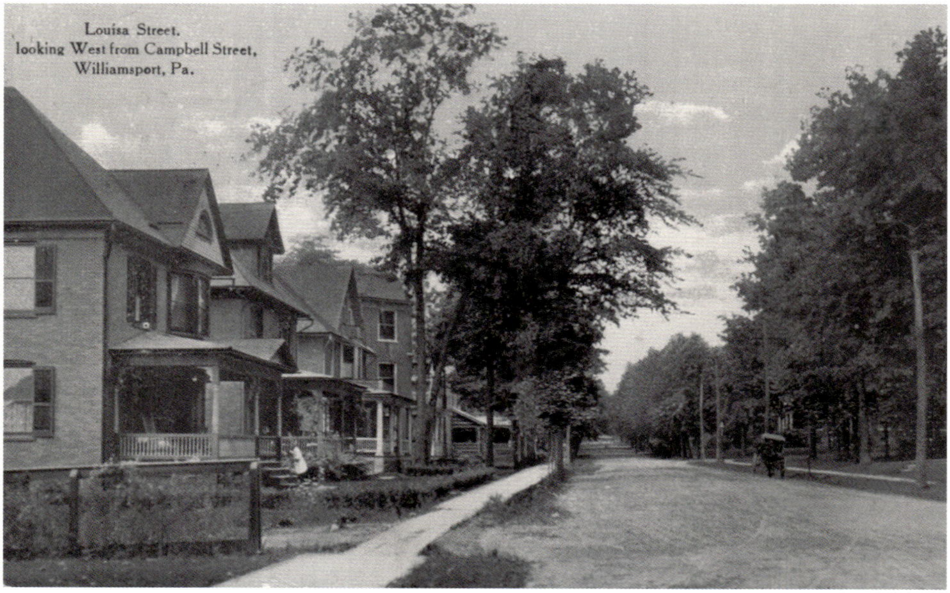

This is the corner of Herdic and Louisa Streets, but when the vintage photograph was taken, around 1910, Herdic Street was just a dirt path. Campbell Street would have been the closest intersection. The first house on the left belonged to the Henry L. Otto family, whose downtown bookstore continues today, though owned by a different family. The little girl running up the steps is probably Agnes Otto, who would have been around five years old at the time.

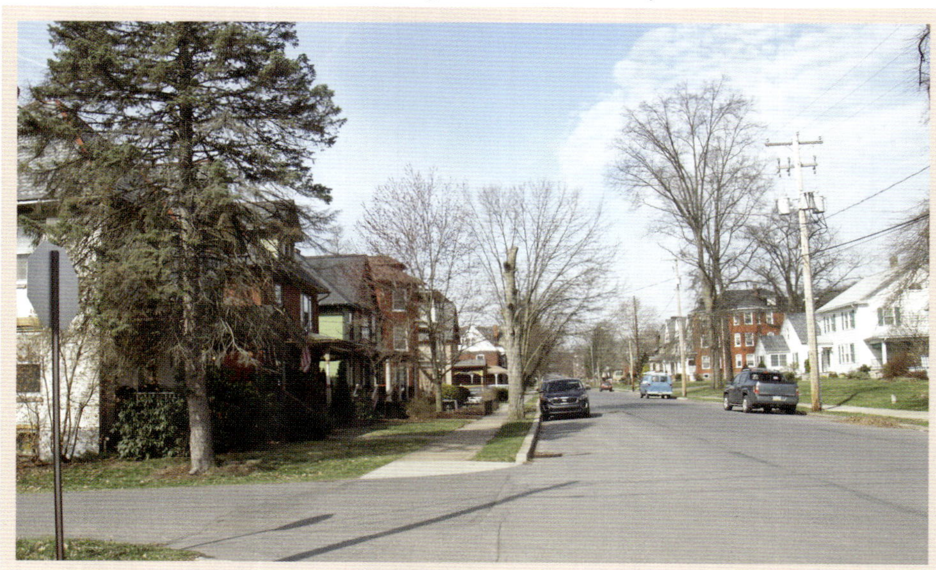

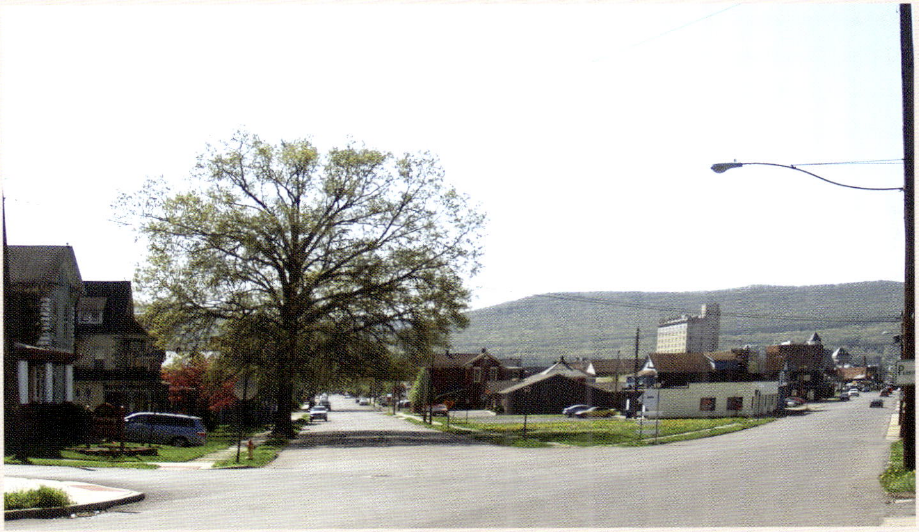

The original plot of Williamsport laid out in 1795 was rectangular, with all streets and alleys crossing each other at right angles. However, around 1815, Andrew Hepburn began expanding the city by laying out plots west of an angled Hepburn Street. The result created intersections such as the one shown here where Pine, Hepburn, and Seventh Streets meet. Several intersections such as this can be seen along Hepburn Street today. (see Confusion Corner on page 12.)

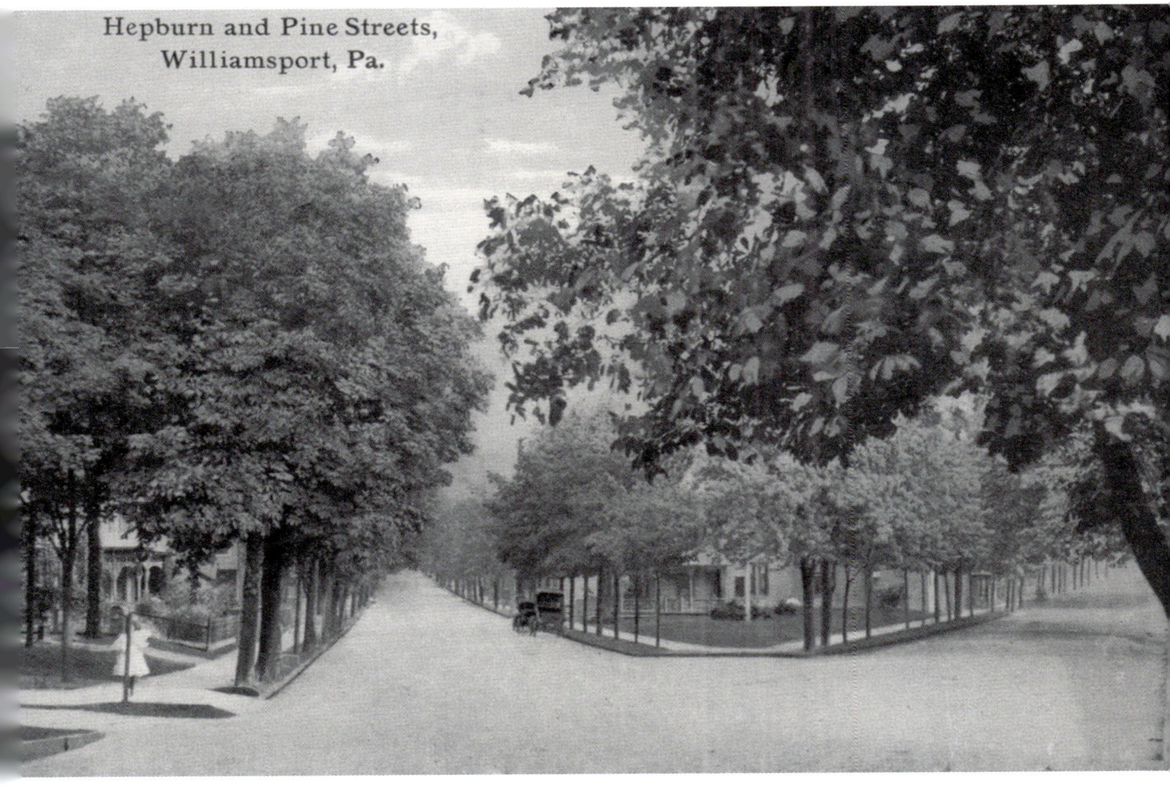

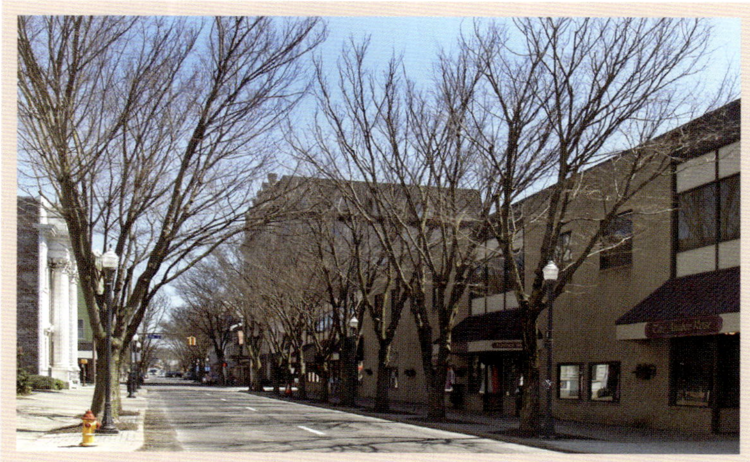

William G. Elliot built the large 208-foot-long and 52-foot-wide, three-story building on the right and opened its second-floor theater in 1870, which was known as the Academy of Music. Large productions and big theater stars of the day performed here. The first floor consisted of several retail shops. After the theater closed around 1893, the second floor was converted into a very successful office space for many years before the building was replaced by a modern structure.

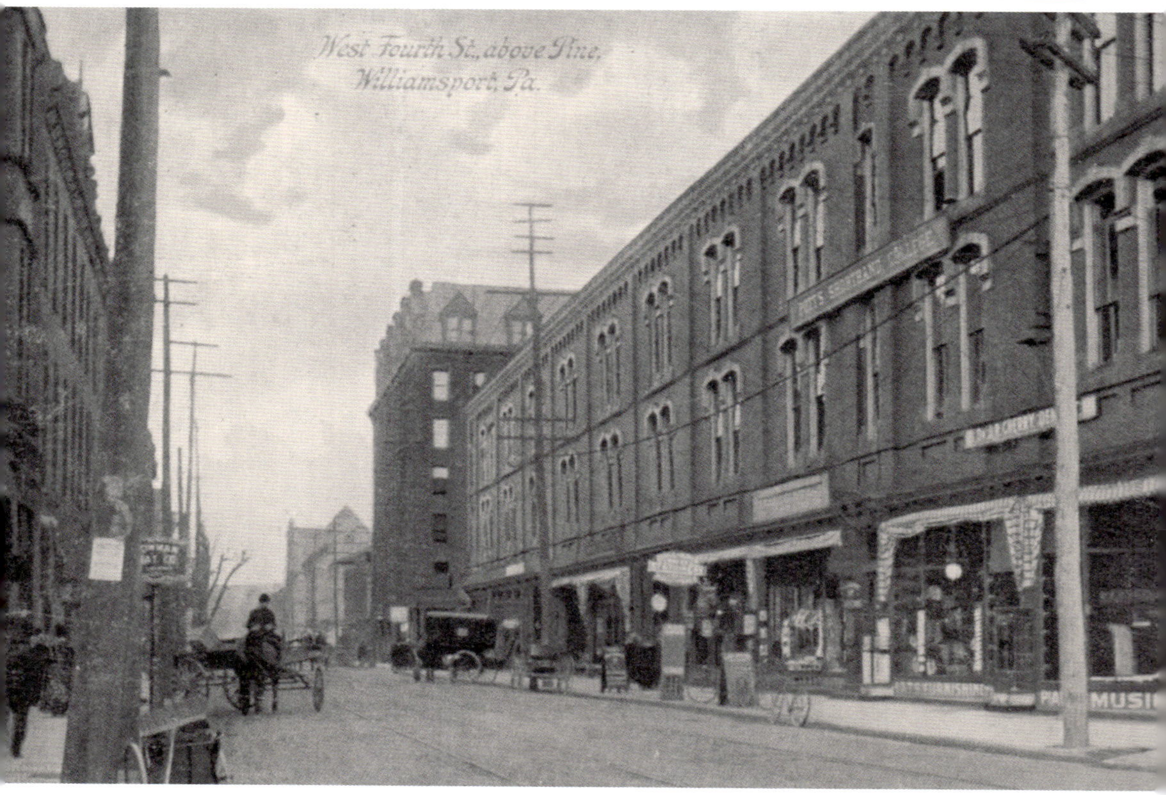

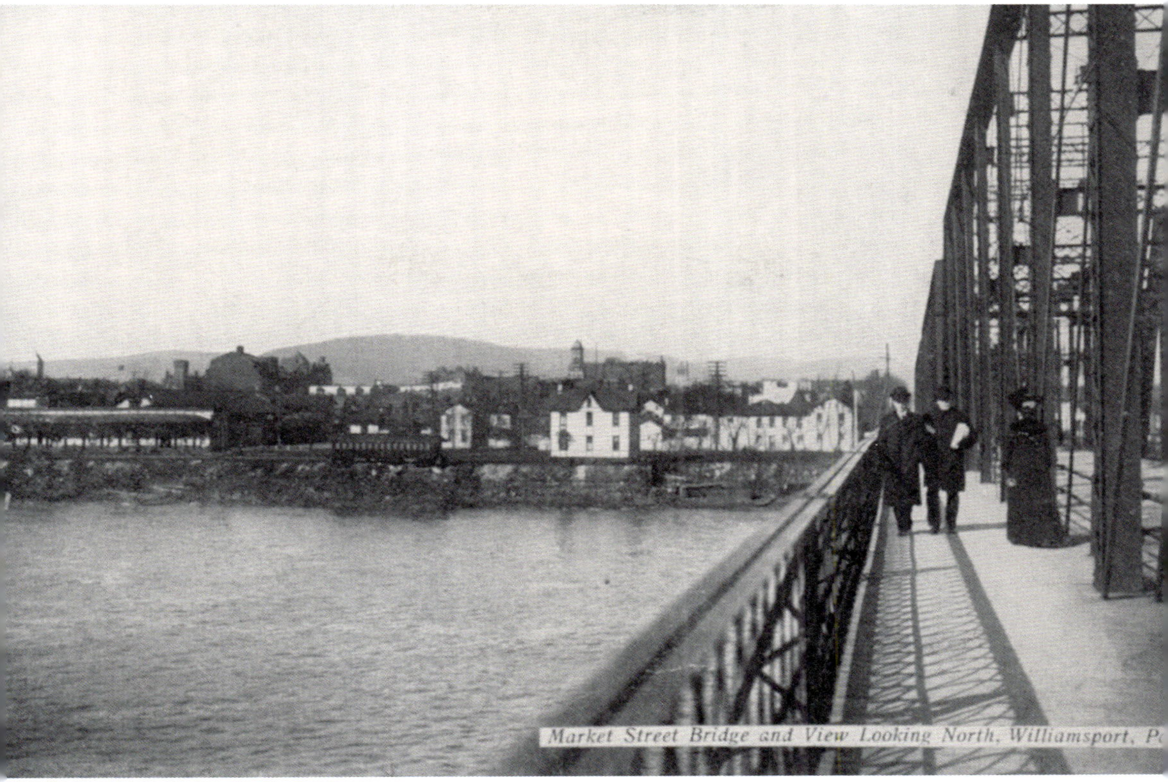

This is a view looking north toward Williamsport from the Carl E. Stotz Memorial Little League Bridge, also known as the Market Street Bridge. Completed in 2007, this is the seventh bridge to span the West Branch of the Susquehanna River between South Williamsport and Williamsport at this location. The first one was wooden covered and opened in 1849. Three more followed. In 1891, the Lycoming County commissioners purchased the bridge, removed the toll, and added a pedestrian walkway.

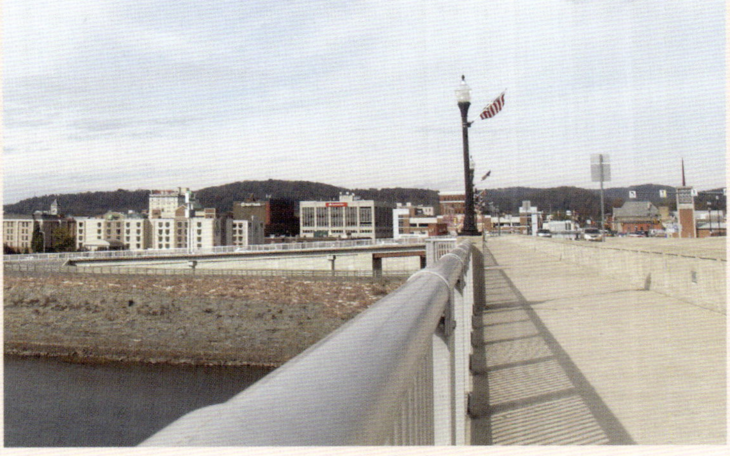

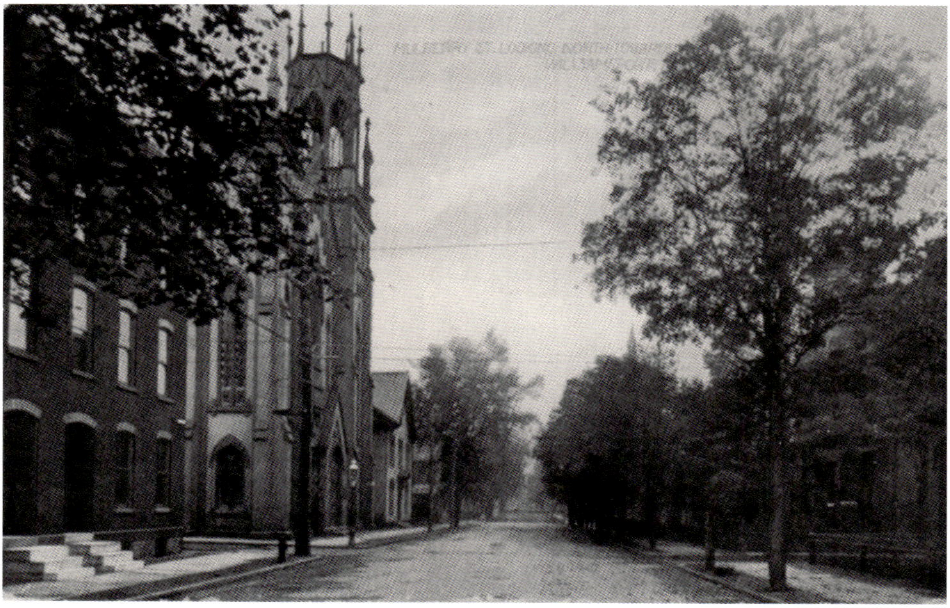

Mulberry Street, in this view looking north at Willow Street and East Fourth Street, was lined with buildings once. The apartment building in the foreground survived until very recently. The house on the corner beyond the church in the c. 1910 postcard was built by James H. Huling and was one of the oldest in the city. The Slate family, leather manufacturers, also resided there for many years. It was torn down in 1970.

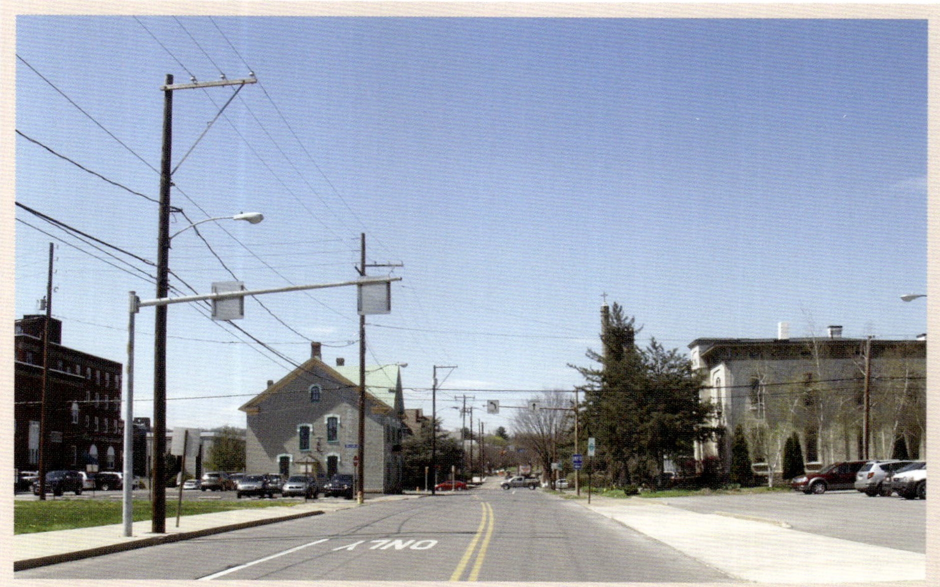

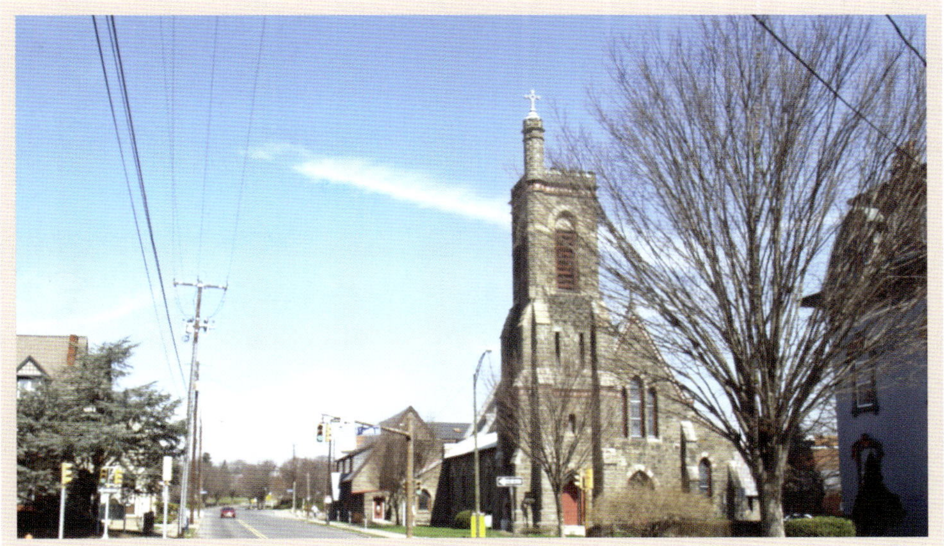

The corner of Mulberry and East Fourth Streets is home to Christ Episcopal Church, organized in 1841. The church building was erected here in 1869, and extensions and additions followed. Among the clergy serving at this church was Rev. Dr. John Henry Hopkins Jr., who wrote the famous Christmas hymn "We Three Kings." Fire House No. 1, now a parking lot, can be seen in the distance along Mulberry Street in the vintage image.

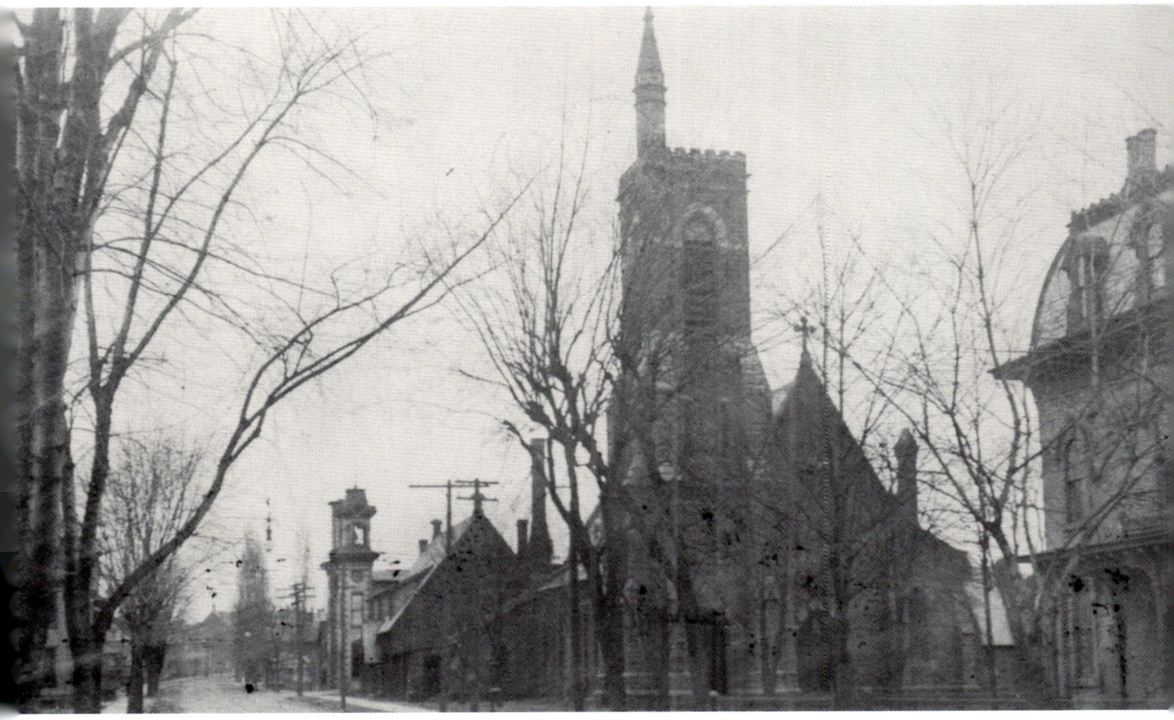

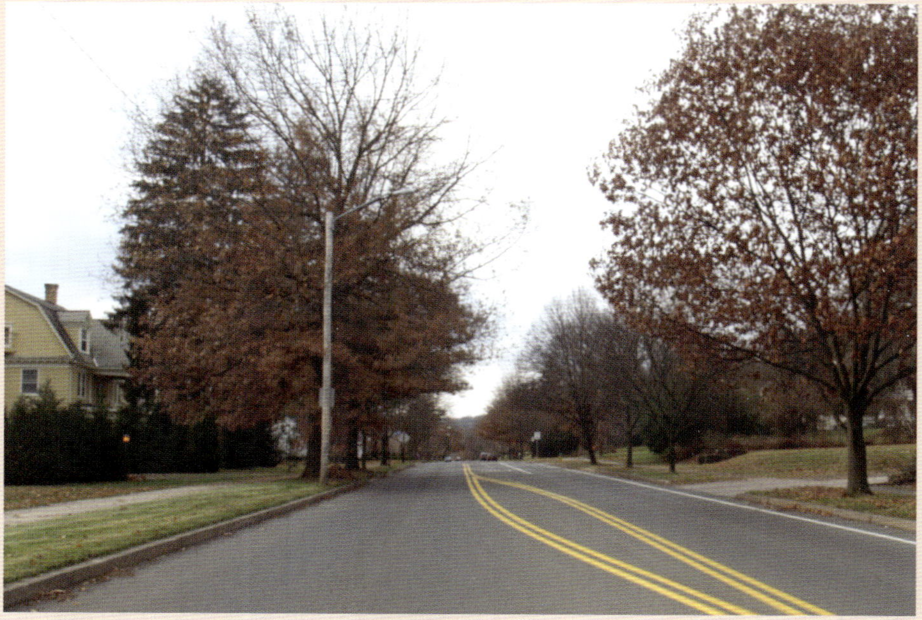

This land, located north of downtown, was laid out with streets and named Grampian Heights by Thomas Lundy's Grampian Land Company beginning in 1892. Trees were planted, sewer lines were laid, and a flat and wide boulevard was created. By 1895, the building boom was underway on Grampian Boulevard. At first, "the Boulevard" was dirt and occasionally served double duty for horse racing. Driving on the paved road today, one can see mansions and beautiful estates on either side.

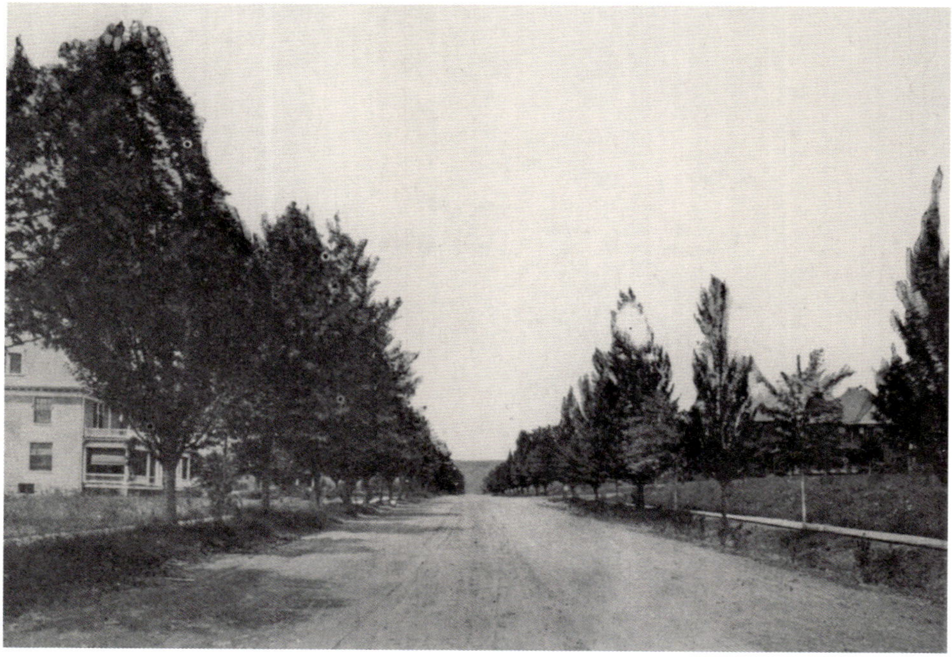

CHAPTER 2

DOWNTOWN

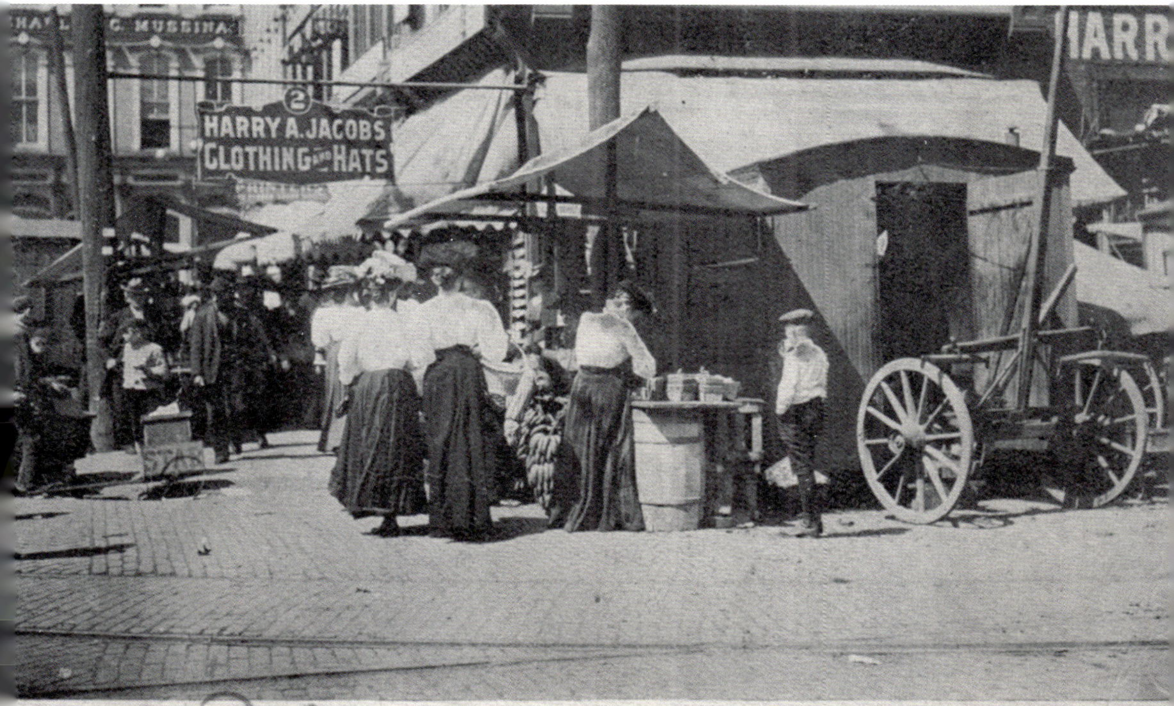

The curbstone market brought many townspeople and merchants together as booths and horse-drawn wagons lined the streets and sidewalks. It was centered at Market Square where Market and Third Streets intersect. Charles Mussina's jewelry store was here on West Third Street in the late 1800s, and the building still stands today.

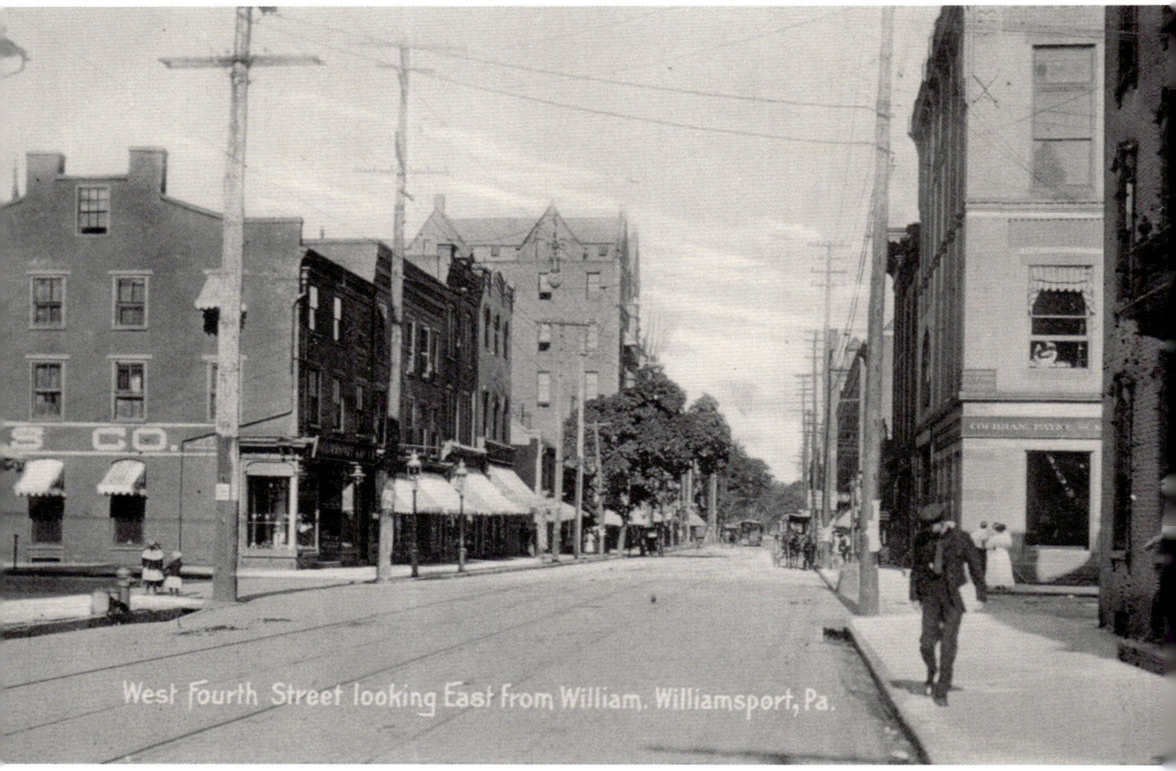

The Williamsport Gas Company building, on the north side of West Fourth Street, center left in both photographs, supplied gas to local residents and businesses. It was in this location from 1899 and had a sales floor that displayed appliances including gas-powered irons, ranges, and gas heaters. The company advertised that all connections were made free, and its heaters were "guaranteed to remove the chill and creepy feeling of a room, even in the coldest weather."

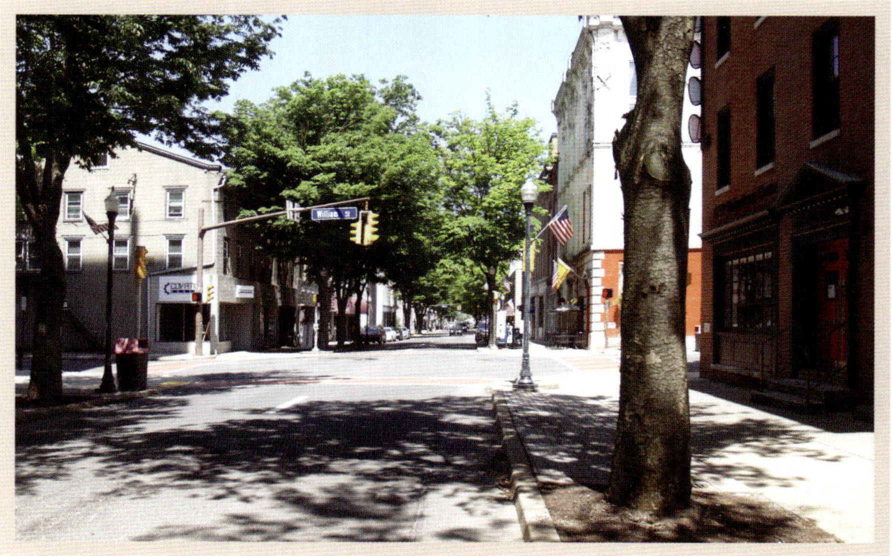

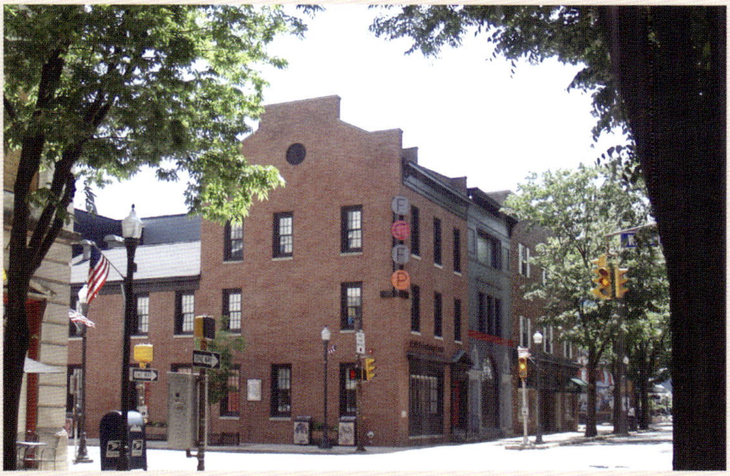

The turn-of-the-century scene of West Fourth Street from William Street looking west shows the Ross Club and the YMCA. West of the YMCA building was Laverty's Patent Medicine store, which offered hair tonic, quinine pills, cod liver oil, and other remedies. Continuing west was the Steam Laundry, a shoemaker, a baker, and a hotel. Across West Alley, modern-day Government Place, was the federal building, which housed the post office. It is now city hall.

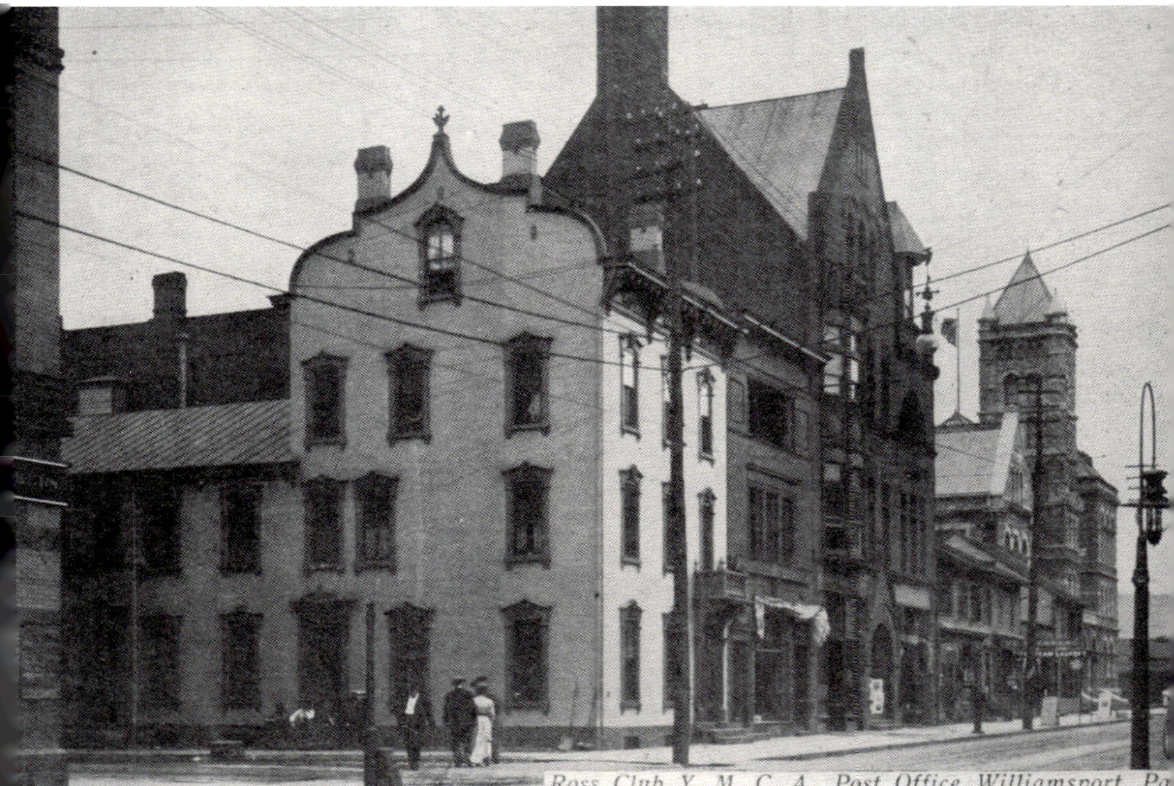

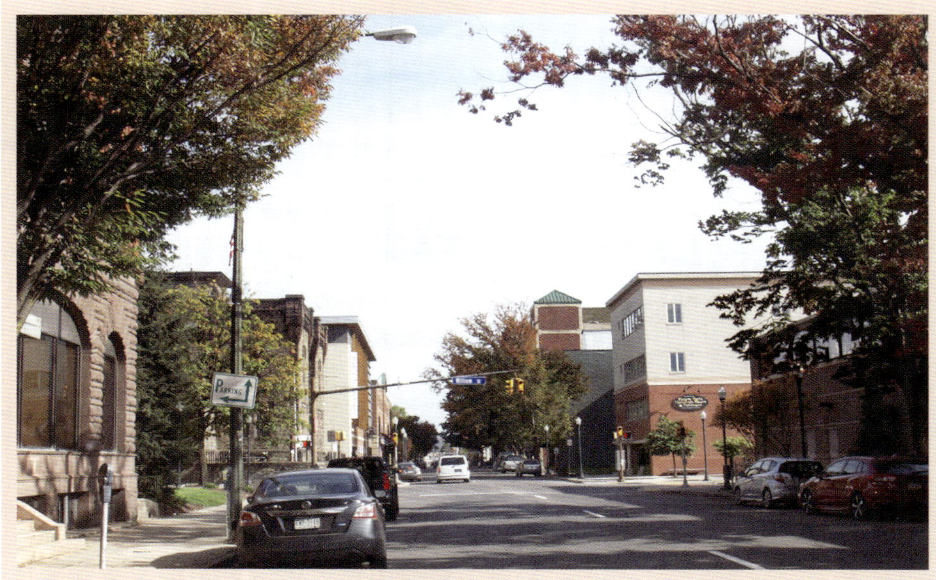

The Grit Building, home of "America's Family Newspaper," can be seen on the left, with bicycles parked in front of it. Bicycle thefts were common, and one was taken from this exact spot in June 1900. The adjacent building was a two-story retail and living space. Henry L. Corter had his electrical supply business here. He sold electrical and gas fixtures, athletic sporting goods, and bicycle supplies. That building is gone today, but the Grit Building remains and houses government offices.

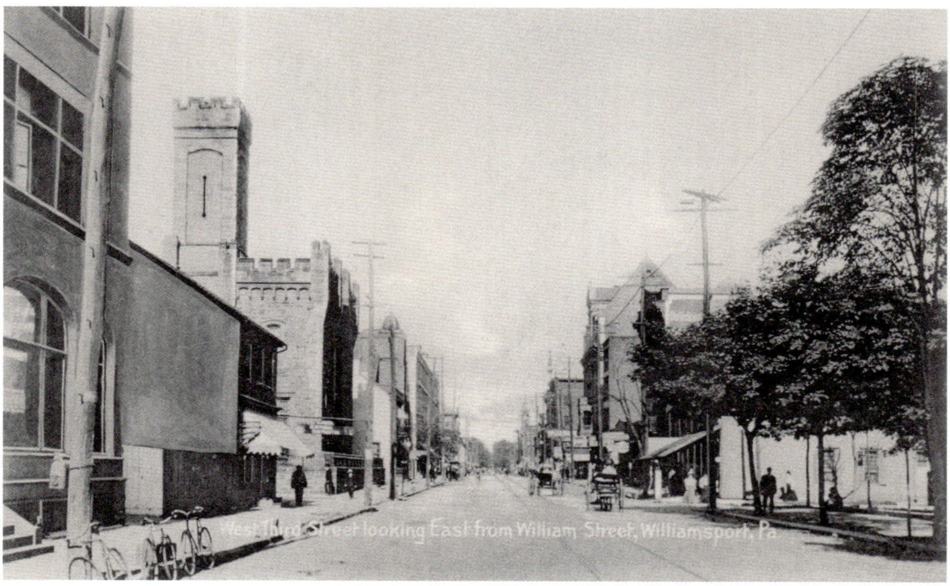

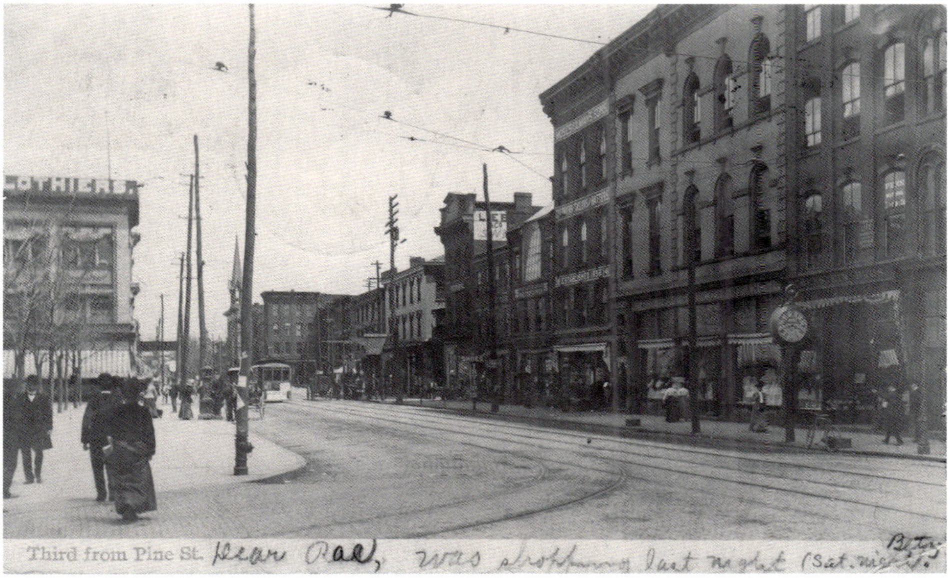

This is a view of West Third Street looking east from Pine Street. In 1893, Rubenstein Bros. opened its Williamsport jewelry store under the charge of George H. Rubenstein, who was killed crossing the street in 1918. The business's clock can be seen in front of the store. Ohrbach's women's clothing store moved into Rubenstein's. The sizeable Bush & Bull dry goods store, the well-known clothier Moses Ulman's Sons, and Irvin's Shoes were adjacent. This entire block has been replaced with a county-owned building.

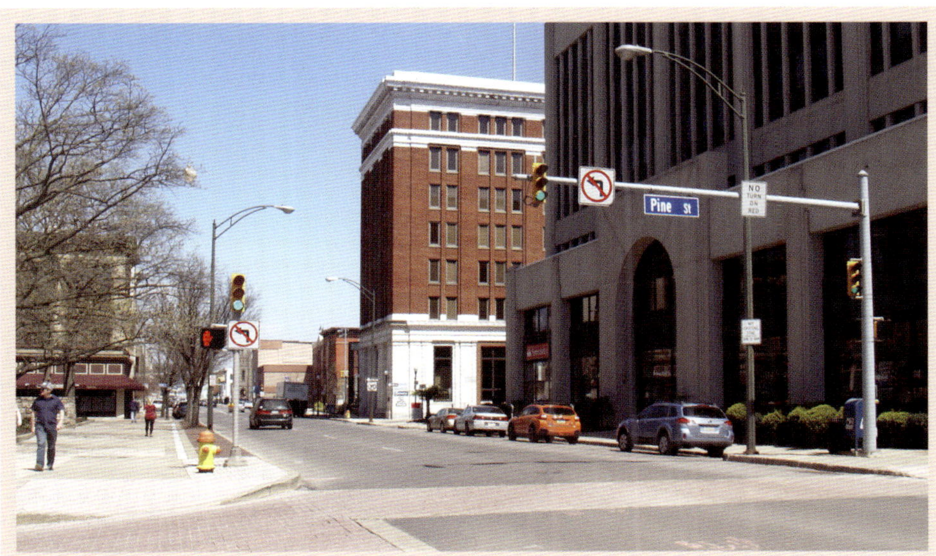

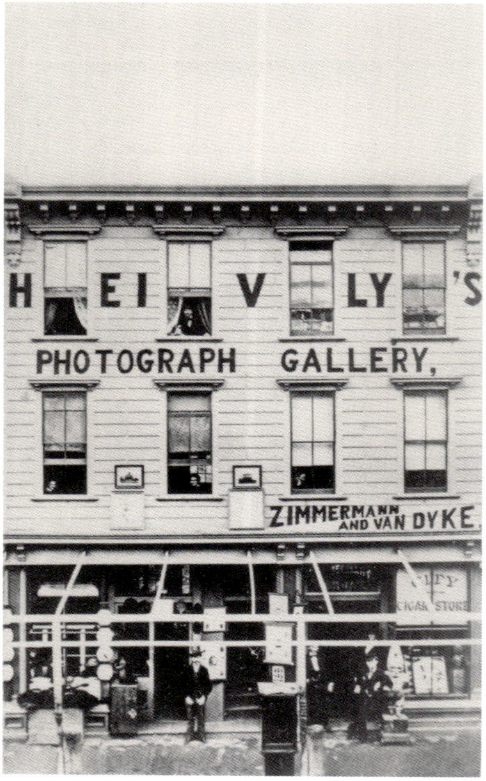

The vintage photograph of this building east of the Hart Building on West Third Street, between Market and Court Streets, was probably taken during or shortly after the 1889 flood. At that time, the first floor was divided into two stores, while the upstairs was a residence and served as a photographic business. As seen here, the left side was a hat and cap store, and the right side was a cigar store.

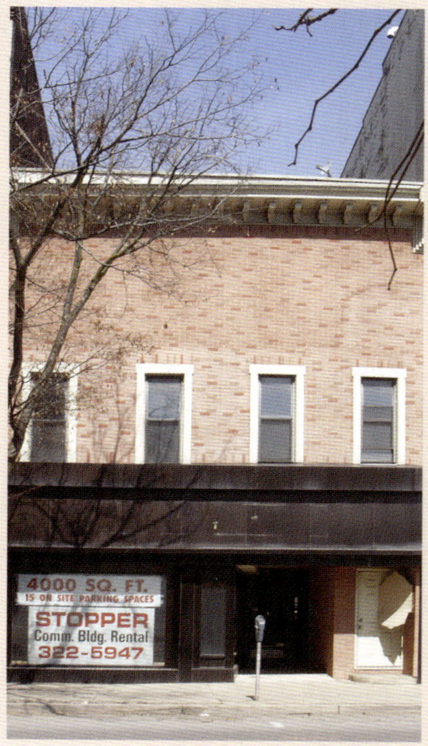

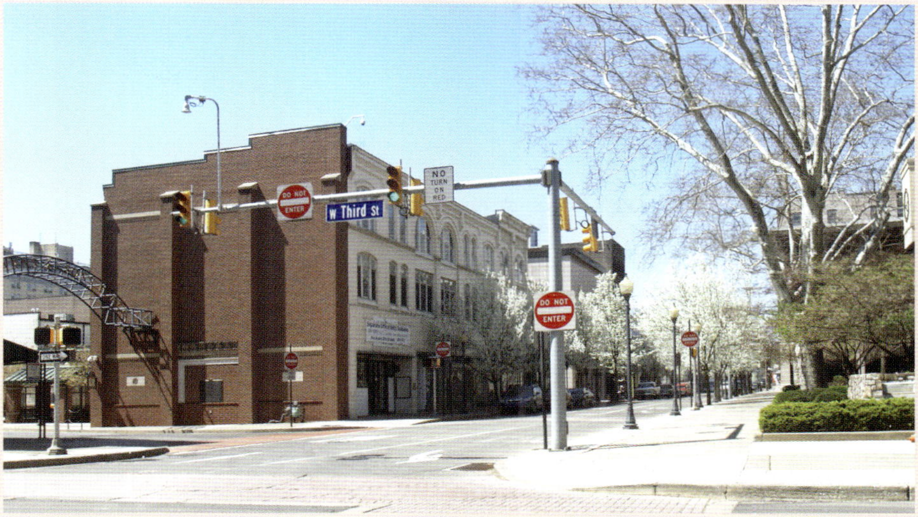

This was the site of City Hotel before L.L. Stearns bought it in 1888 to relocate his store from Market Square. When West Branch National Bank moved to West Fourth Street in 1917, Stearns purchased the bank's previous location and eventually expanded into that building. Today, LL Stearns & Sons Plaza, a picturesque transportation terminal, commemorates one of the largest and most popular stores Williamsport has ever seen.

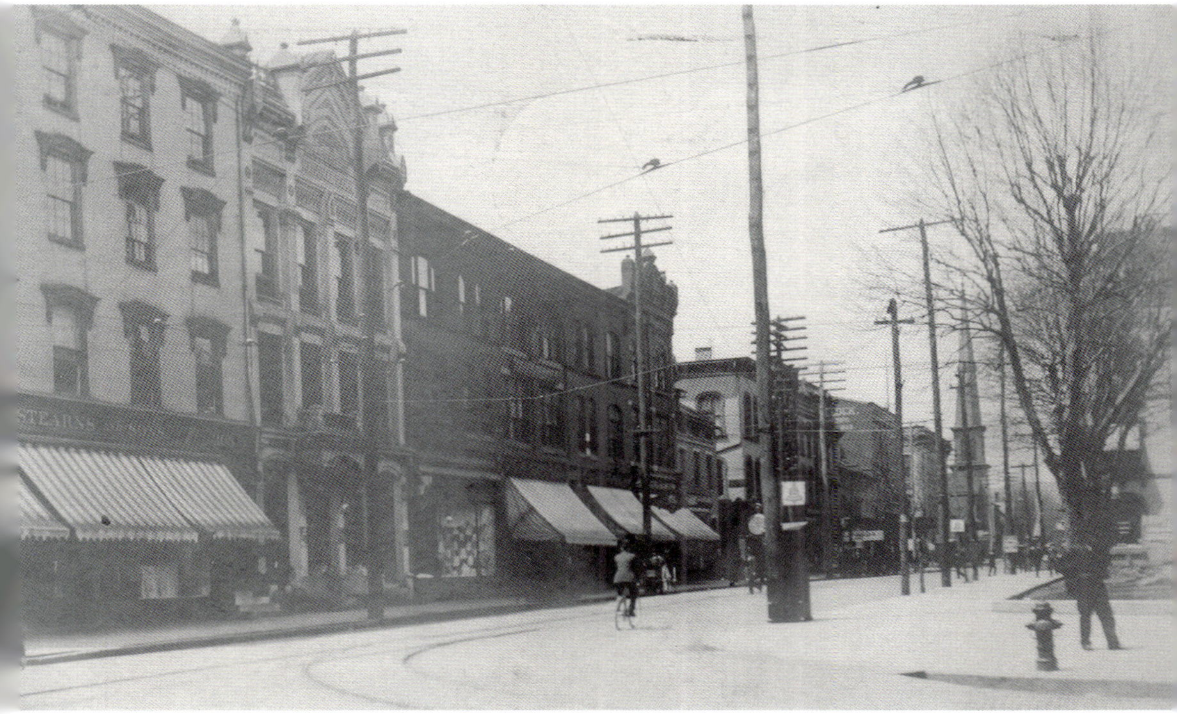

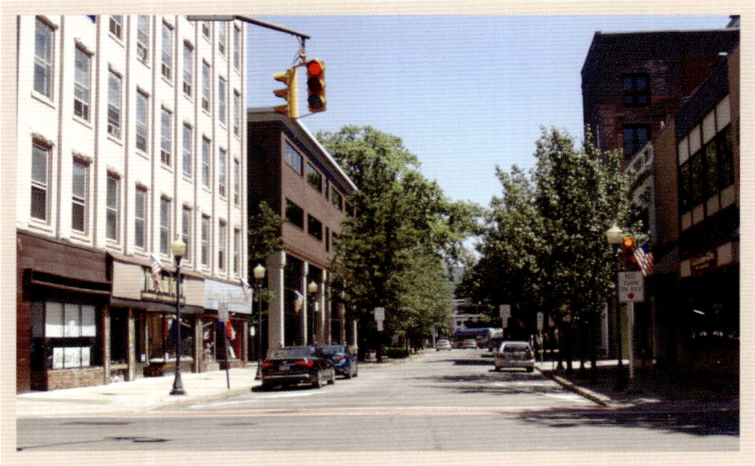

Pine Street between Fourth and Willow Streets held an eclectic assortment of shops and services including two banks, a dry goods store, a telegraph office, and a sporting-goods store. Many of these buildings still survive today. Rexall, Millener Drug Co., on the corner, sold a variety of items including candy, ice cream, and tickets to local events but specialized in a large selection of remedies. In 1911, the window display had live venomous snakes to promote Worner's Famous Rattlesnake Oil.

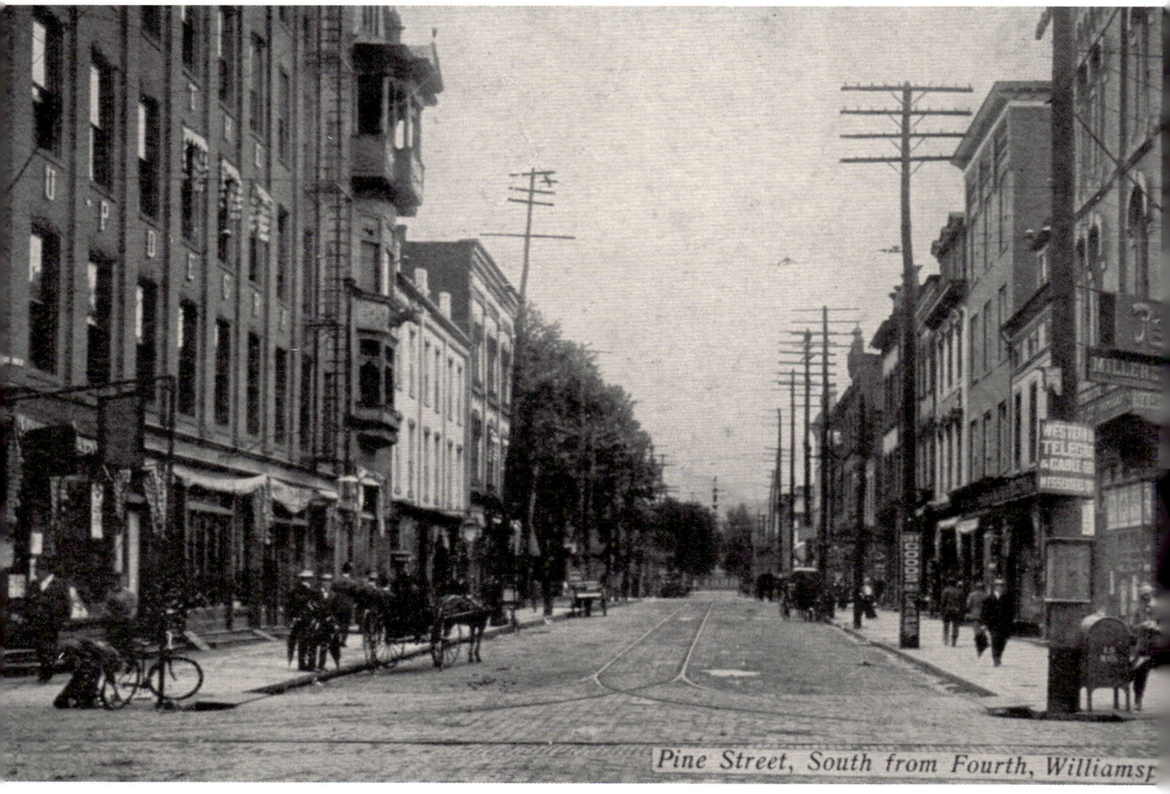

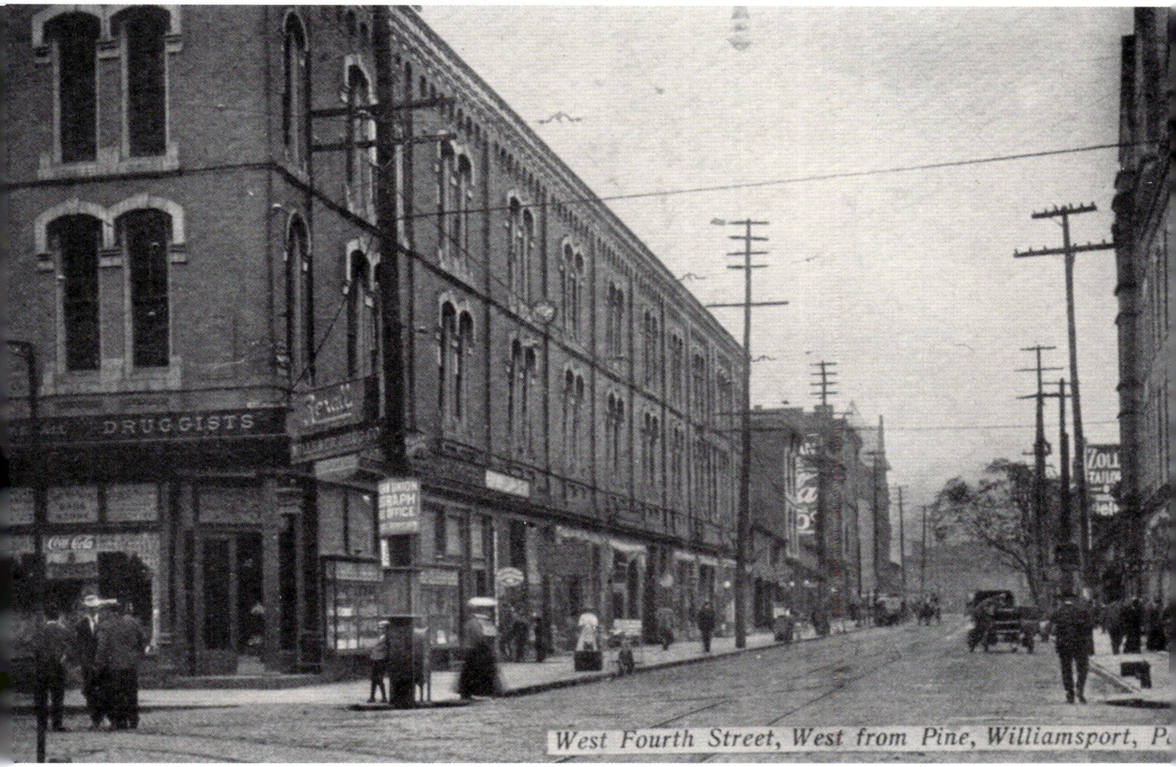

Looking west on West Fourth Street, the Academy of Music building dominates the vintage scene above. Beyond it is Laurel Street where, at the corner, a two-story wood frame building stood. It served as several saloons through the years. It was replaced by a three-story brick building, which is no longer standing. Instead, Laurel Street is wider. The next building, which is still standing, was a series of hotels and then retail stores, and is currently Kinley Jewelers.

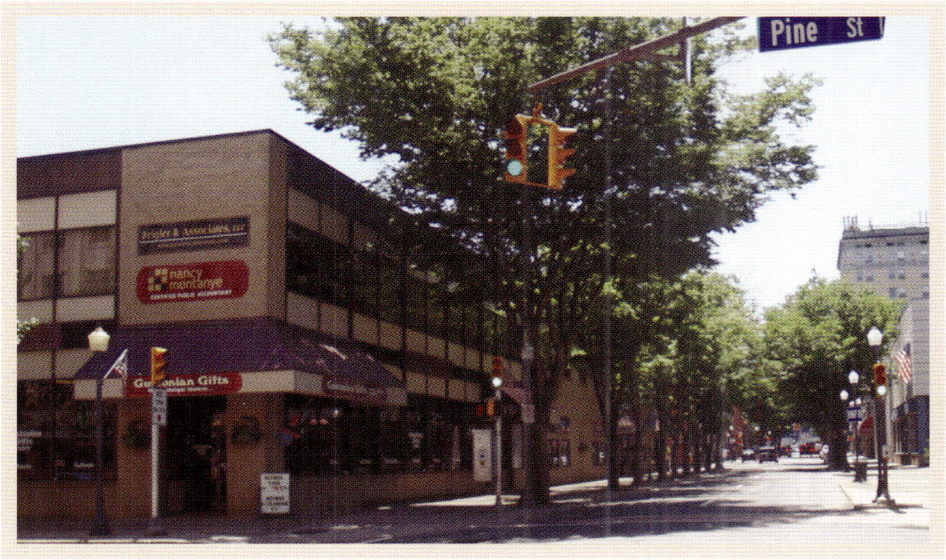

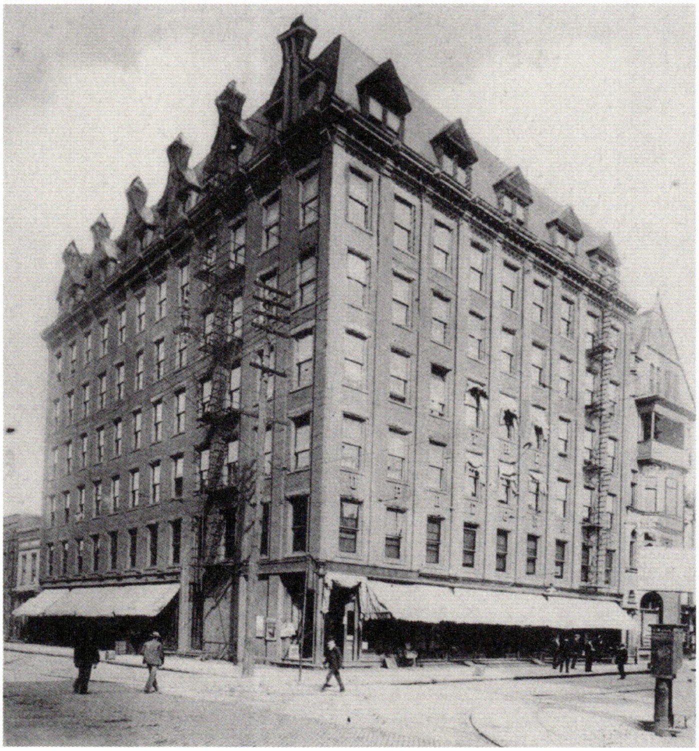

The Updegraff Hotel was built in 1891–1892. Elevators were not as safe as they are now, and at least twice, the elevator at the Updegraff went out of control. Once, in 1908, it ascended with great force to the roof, and another time, in 1911, it slid slowly to the bottom. It was not occupied either time. Though the upper portion of the original 150-room hotel has been converted to apartments, the exterior is remarkably unchanged.

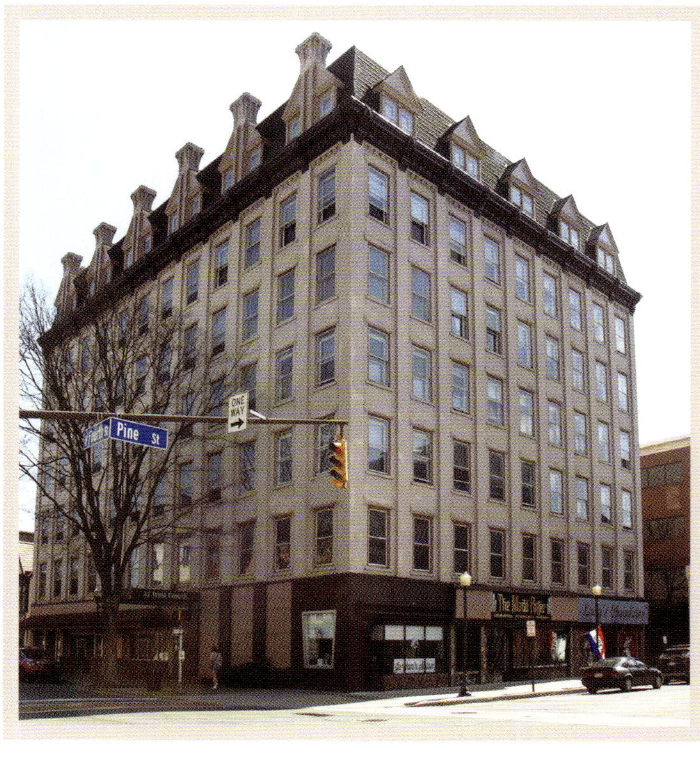

CHAPTER 3

BUSINESSES AND INDUSTRIES

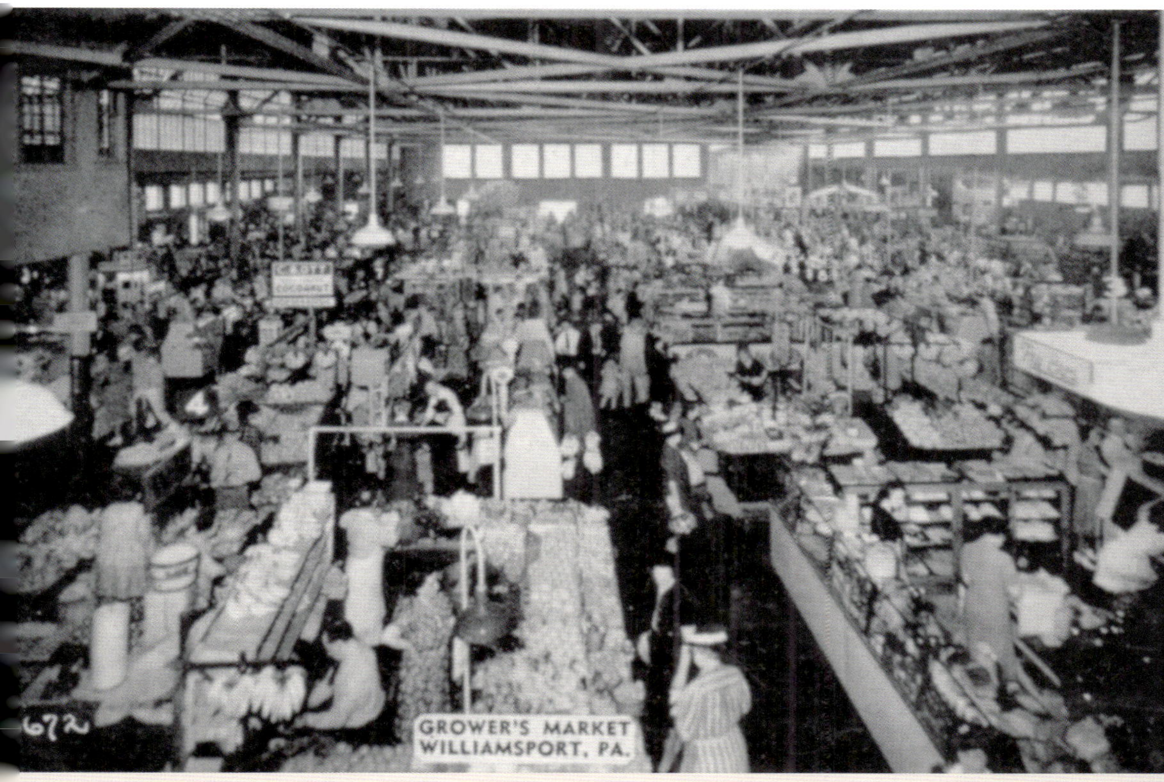

Fruit, vegetables, meat, fish, poultry, flowers, and many other items could be purchased, all under one roof, at the Growers Market on Market Street. Evolving from the outdoor curbstone market, this indoor market was very popular and thrived from the 1930s until it closed in 1973.

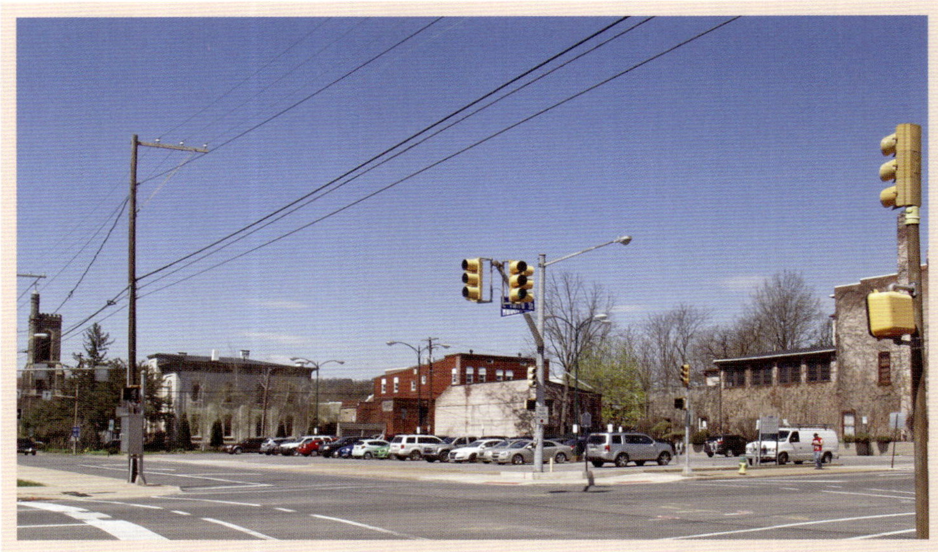

The northeast corner of East Third and Mulberry Streets, at times referred to as the Commercial Block, was an important place of business. In the c. 1906 photograph below, Guy Jarrett's drugstore can be seen on the corner. Next to that was Amos Mertz's furniture store, later becoming Kaplan Bros., and next to that was the very successful Williamsport Macaroni Manufacturing Company, which made and sold different kinds of pasta, ice-cream cones, and imported fruits. This corner is a parking lot now.

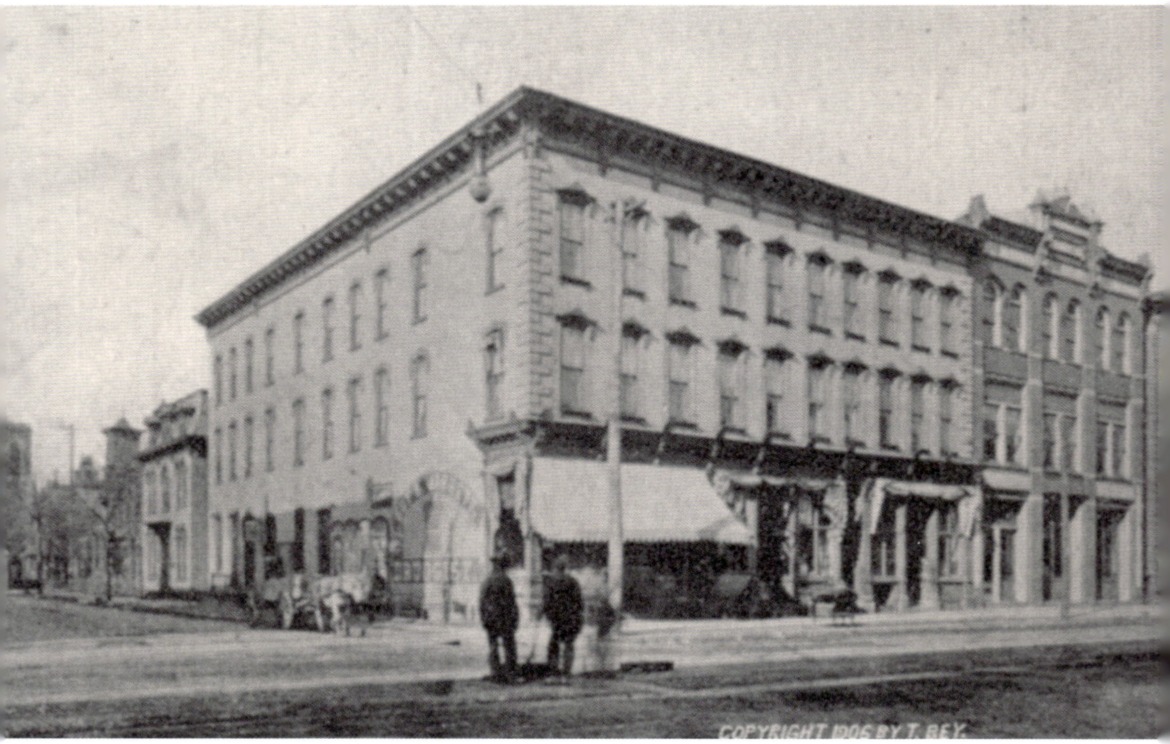

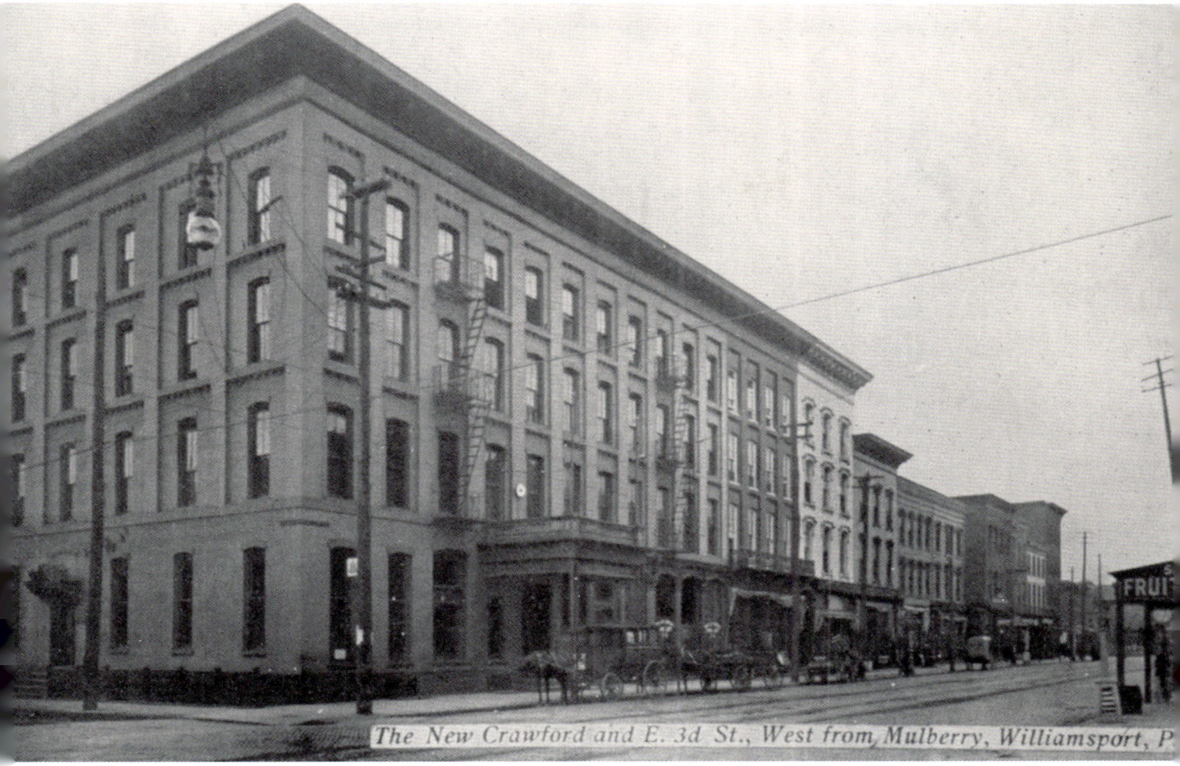

The New Crawford Hotel was just one name this building knew in its lifetime. It also went by Porter House, Hotel Crawford, the Walford, Hotel Hicks, and the Gates Hotel before it became a dormitory and headquarters for the Williamsport YWCA around 1912. In 1931, shortly after the YWCA moved out, it partially collapsed. After that, what was left of it became a bus terminal. Today, it is an empty grass lot.

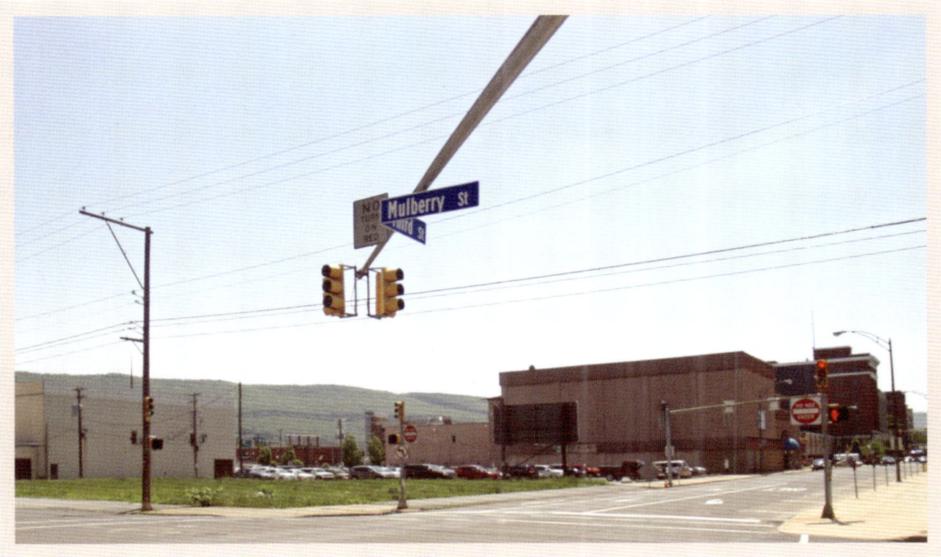

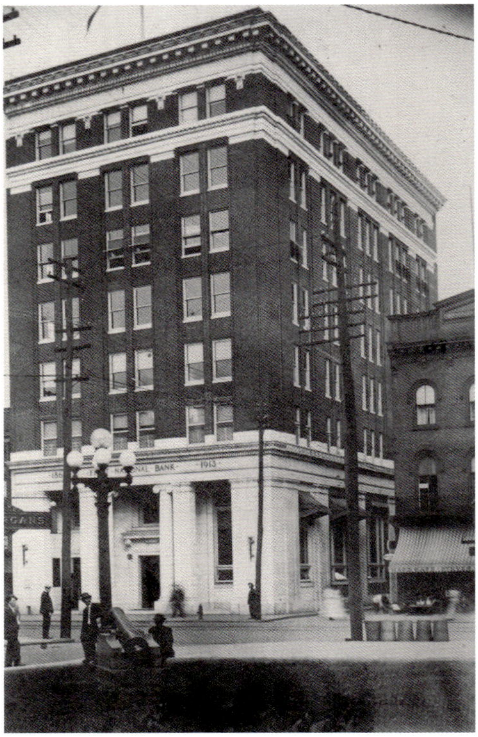

This West Third Street building was constructed during the 50th anniversary of First National Bank. Now Penn Towers, in 1913, it replaced the former three-story bank building on this same spot. It was built to have the entire first floor for banking; the top six floors were intended for offices. Caen stone, white marble, and Tiffany & Co light fixtures were employed in the design. Bronze Tiffany gates continue to guard one of the entrances.

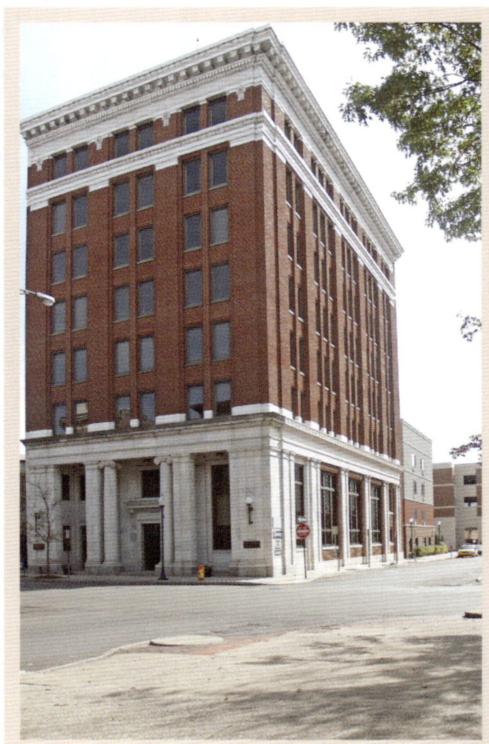

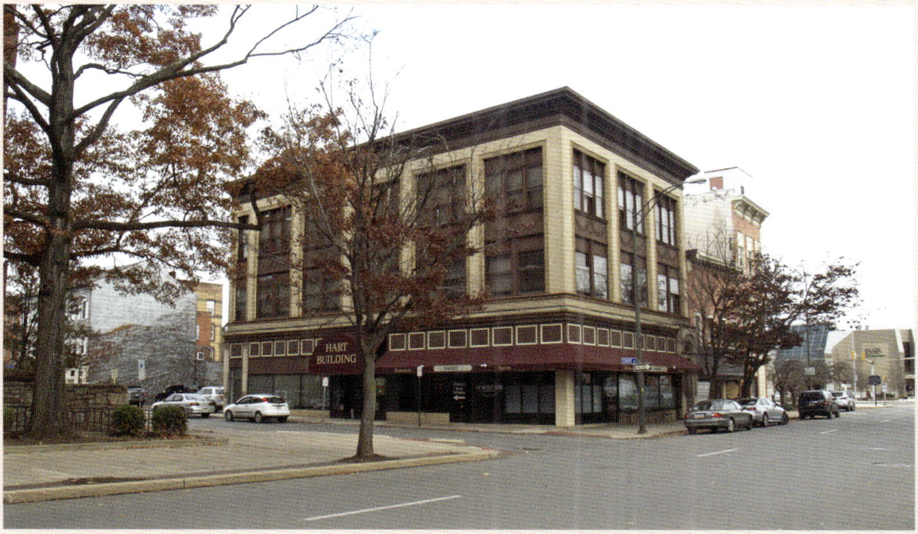

Mayor William G. Elliot, who built Elliot's Academy of Music, watched as his boyhood home on the corner of Third and Court Streets was torn down on July 15, 1895. In good spirits, he said, "I like to see progress." By December of that year, the new and larger Hart Building, seen here, was open for business. To offer the best indoor light, Amos Hart chose to surround the entire first floor with plate-glass windows.

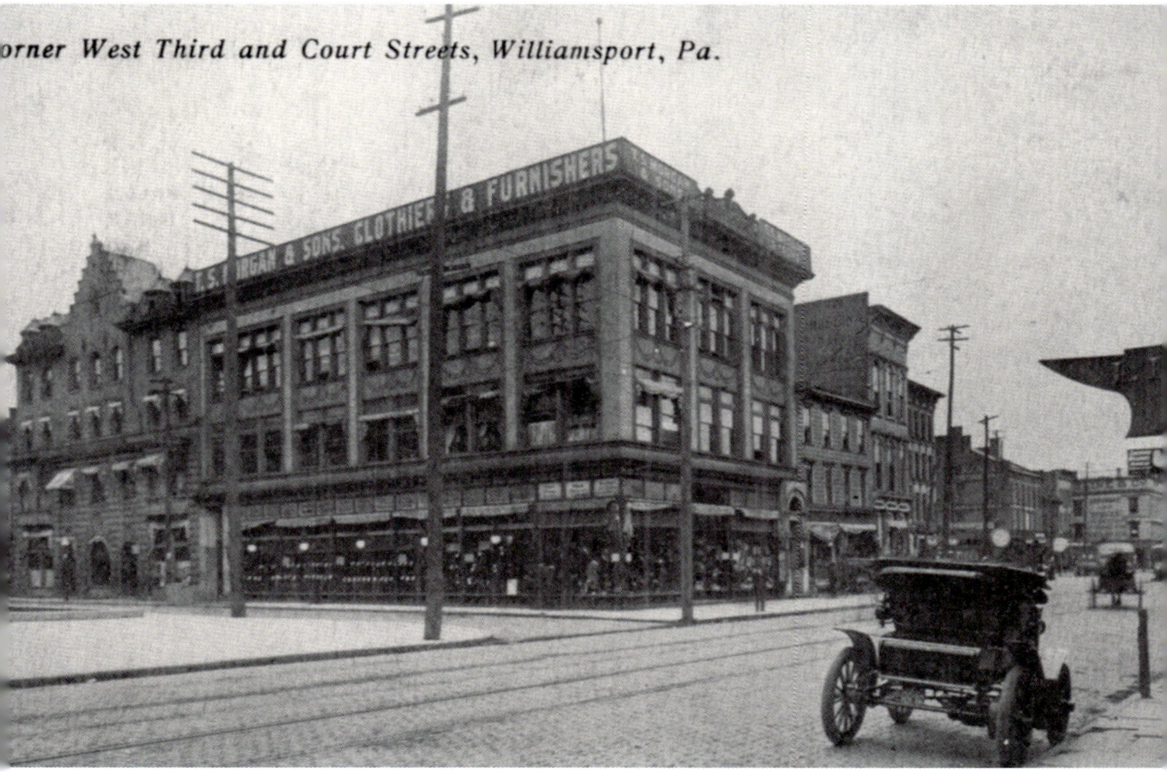

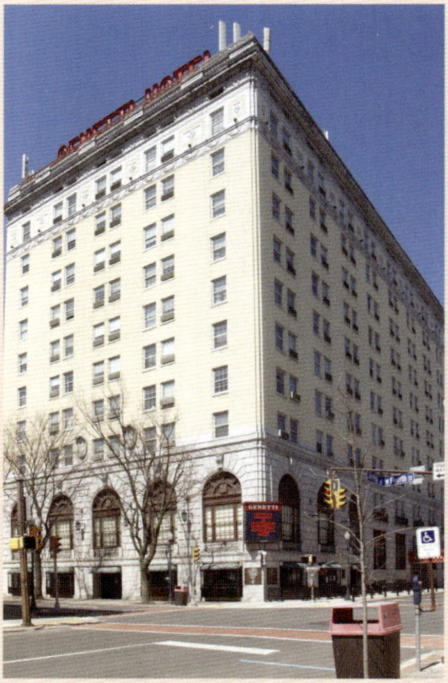

The impressive 10-story Lycoming Hotel opened on June 22, 1922, with 212 guest rooms, at a cost of over $1 million. Sixteen-foot ceilings graced the luxurious lobby, which led into the main dining room to the right of the William Street entrance. There were also four private dining rooms, a ballroom, cafeteria, soda fountain, and barbershop. It proudly featured two Otis self-leveling electric passenger elevators and a 100-car garage. Today, as the Genetti Hotel, it maintains its 1922 elegance.

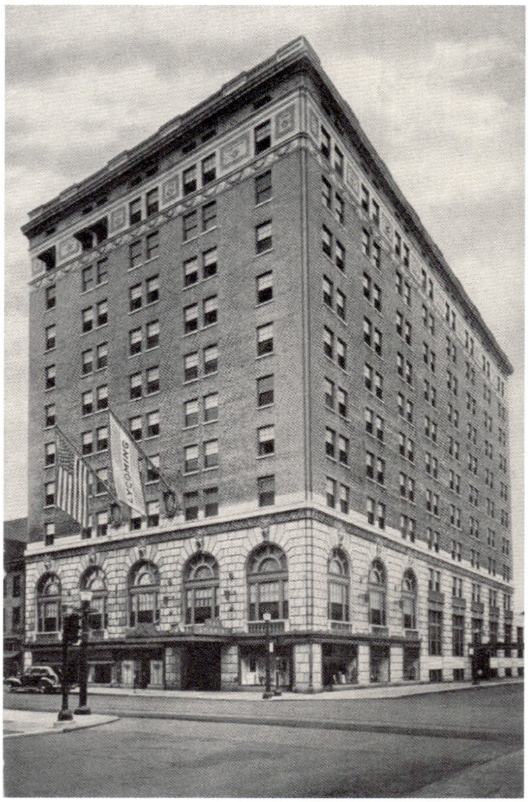

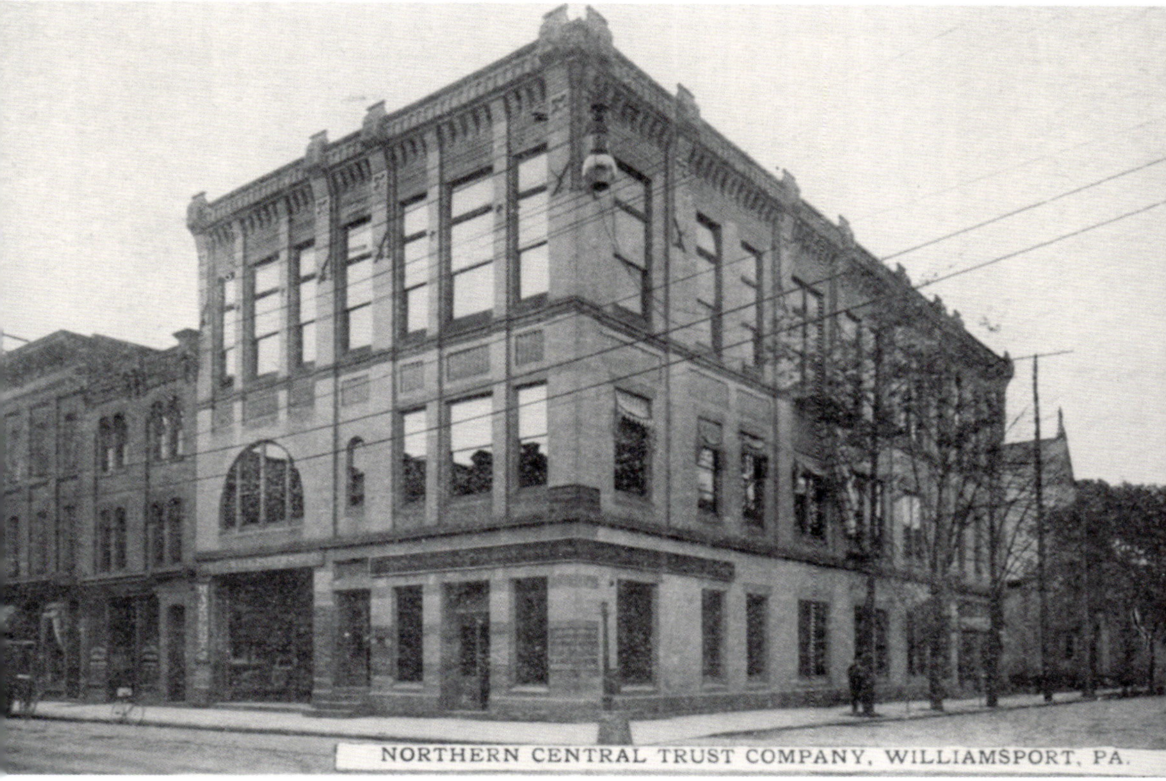

The c. 1909 photograph above shows Northern Central Trust at 153 West Fourth Street. The trust company opened on August 2 of that year, taking over the Cochran, McCormick & Cochran bank at that same location. Much later, this was known as the Arcade Building. The adjoining business on the left was the Hazelet Wallpaper and Art store. Except for the arrangement of doors and windows on the first floor, the exterior remains much the same.

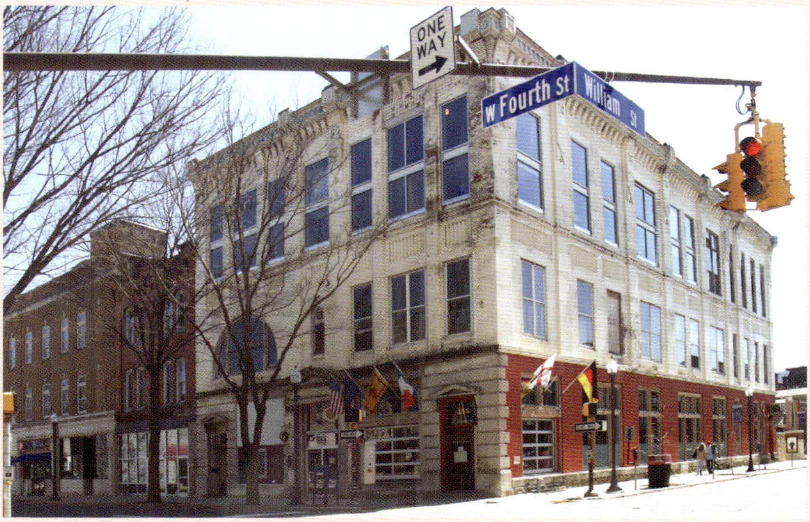

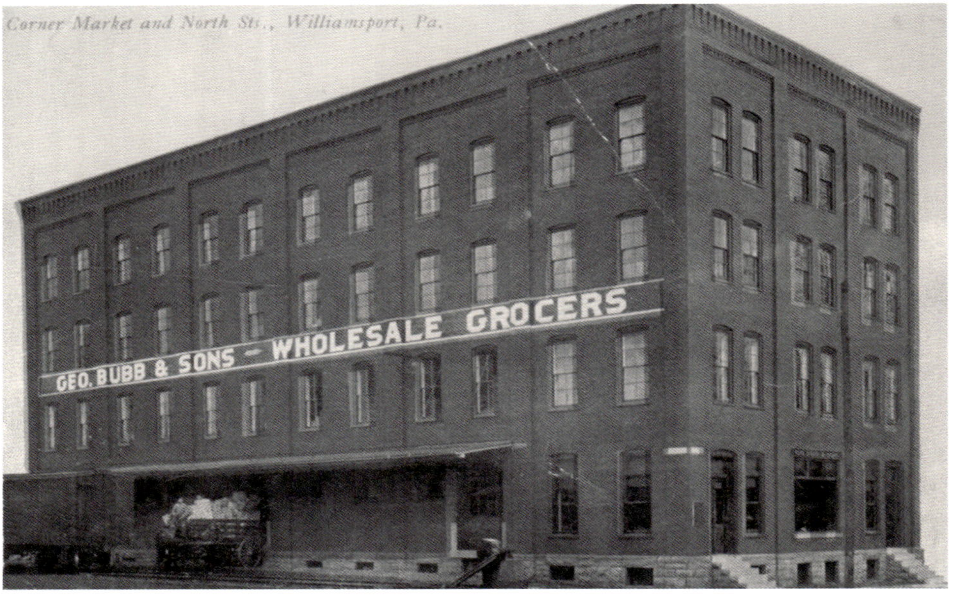

To accommodate its growing need for space, George Bubb & Co. grocery wholesaler relocated to a newly built warehouse at 460 Market Street in 1910, now an office building. A switch of the Pennsylvania railroad was built next to it for the convenient unloading of freight. On May 23, 1911, a public exhibit was offered featuring tours of the facility. Over 500 people attended and were given lunch in an impromptu dining room on the third floor.

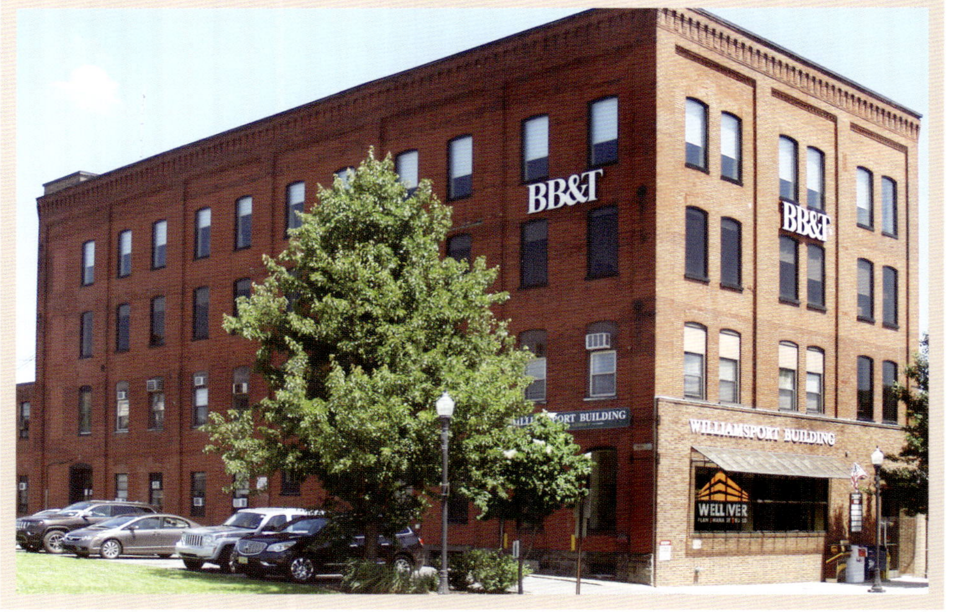

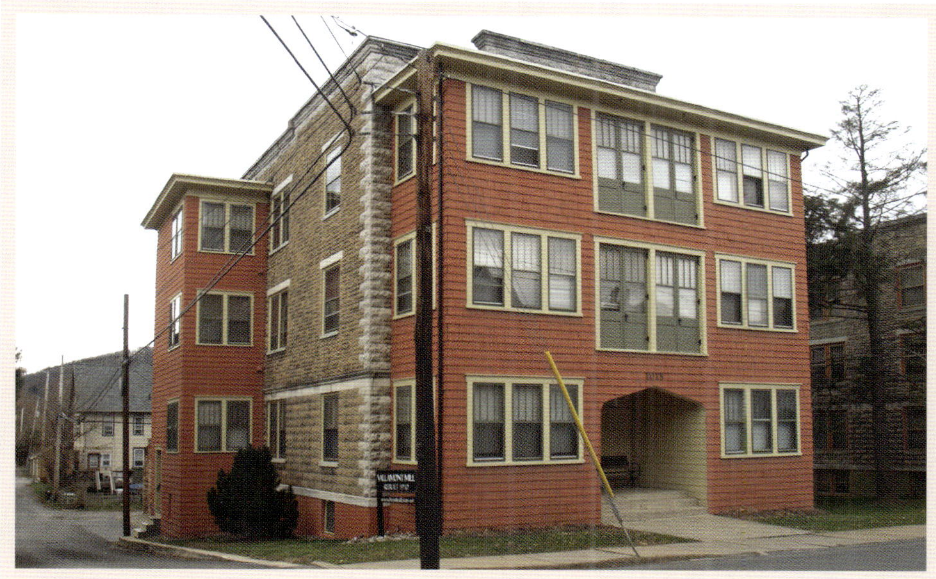

The Vallamont Building and Planing Mill Company constructed this three-story building at 1015 Market Street in 1910 to replace an earlier mill building. This company is responsible for more than 500 structures in Williamsport and the surrounding area as well as the decorative lumber of many buildings built by others. In 1927, after the company relocated from this site, it converted the mill into apartments with porches and balconies. The apartments have been restored to their 1920s appearance.

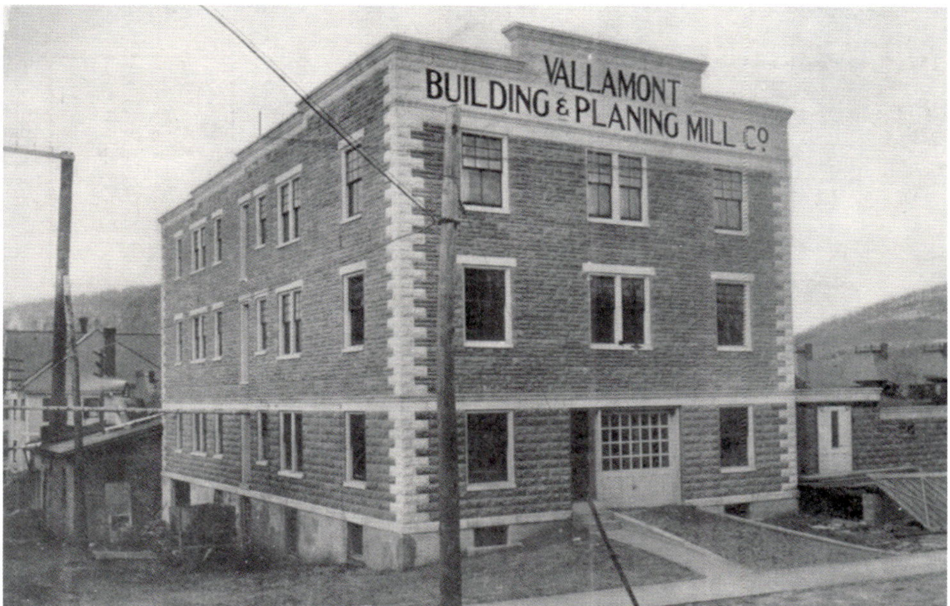

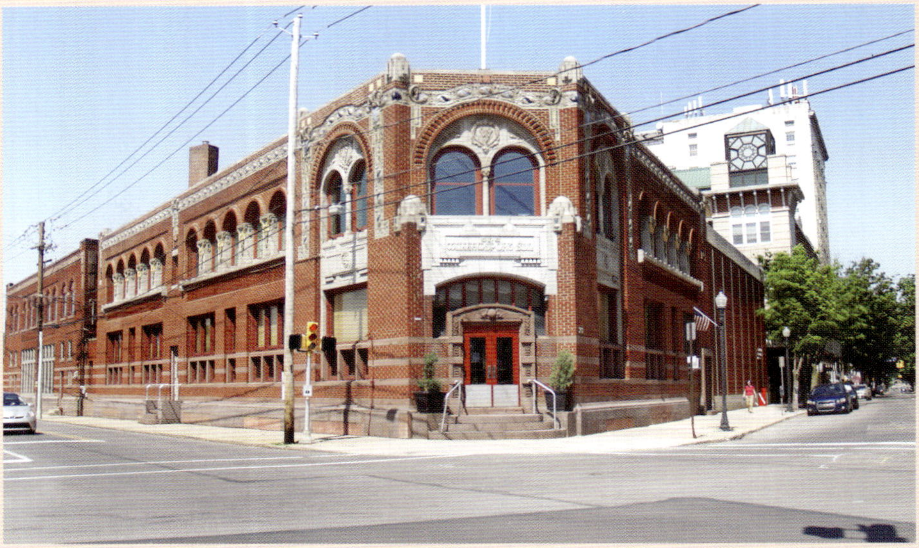

In 1906, this property was purchased by the *Williamsport Sun.* Said to be the highest plot of ground in the city at the time, it was conveniently located near the post office and railroad stations. It took the paper a few years to move into its new home, but it has been there ever since. In 1955, the *Sun* and the *Gazette & Bulletin* consolidated to become the *Williamsport Sun-Gazette.*

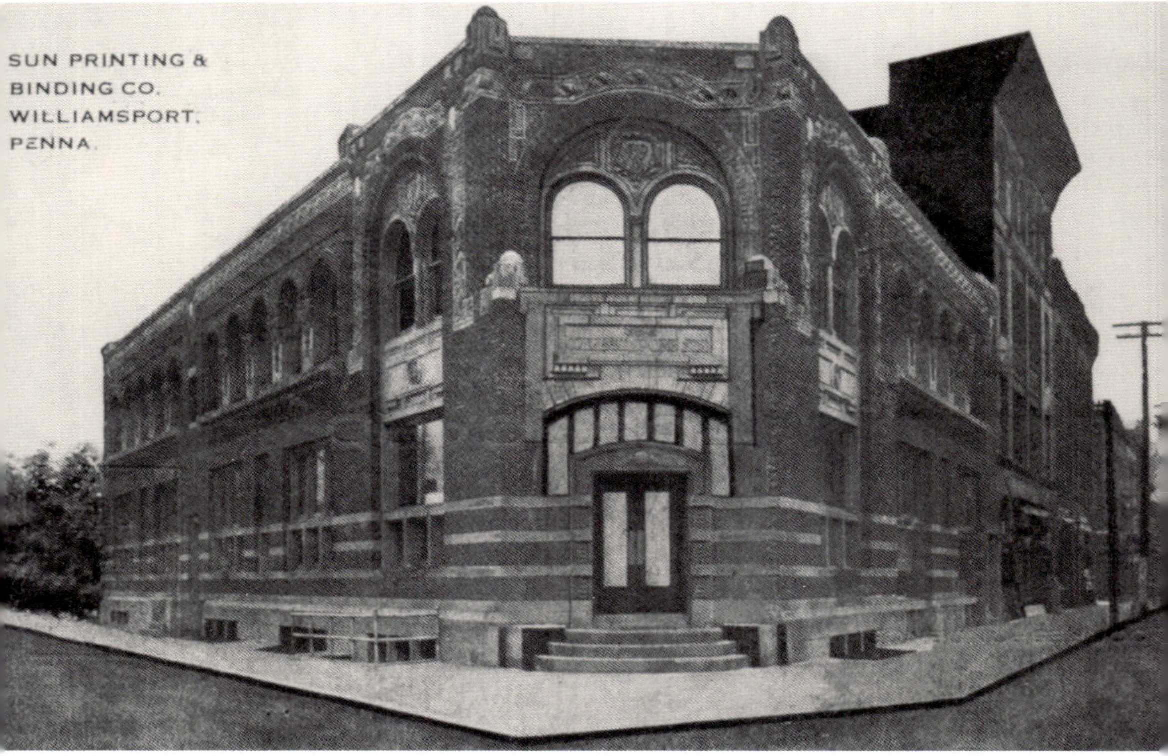

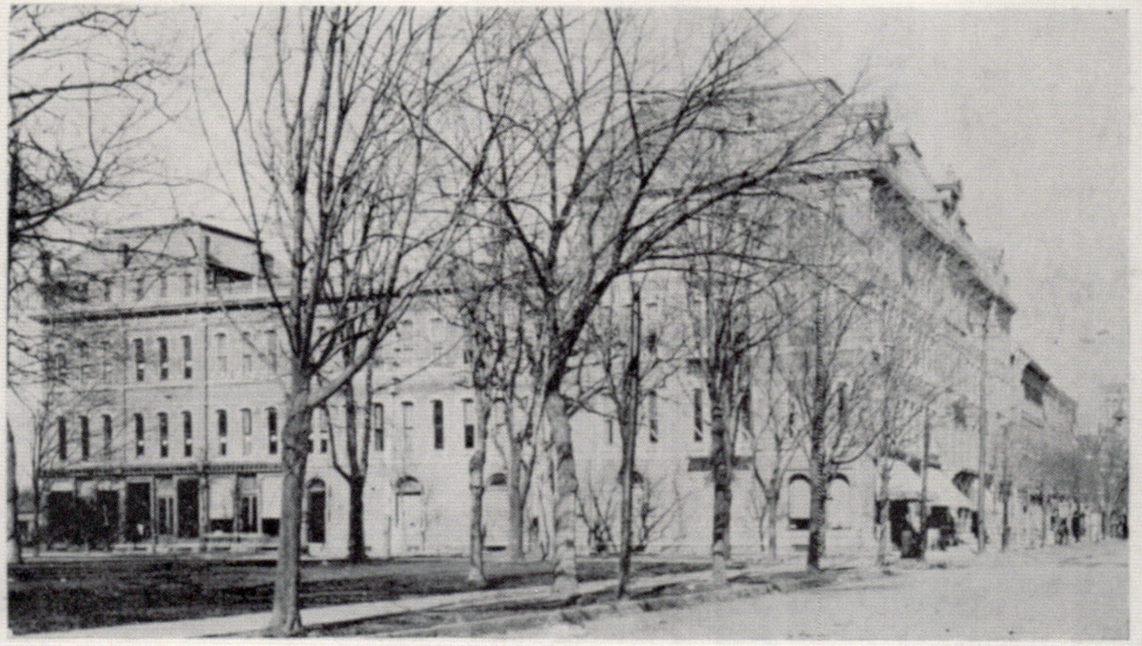

Weightman Block, Fourth and Campbell Sts., Williamsport, Pa.

This U-shaped building on the corner of Campbell and Fourth Streets was Peter Herdic's dream, but he went bankrupt in 1878 before it could be fully realized. What he started as the Herdic Building became the Weightman Building. One of the first occupants was the Self-Locking Suspender Company, which started in 1890. There was also a drugstore, grocer, and dry goods store here at that time. Numerous improvements have recently been made, including updates to the upper-floor apartments.

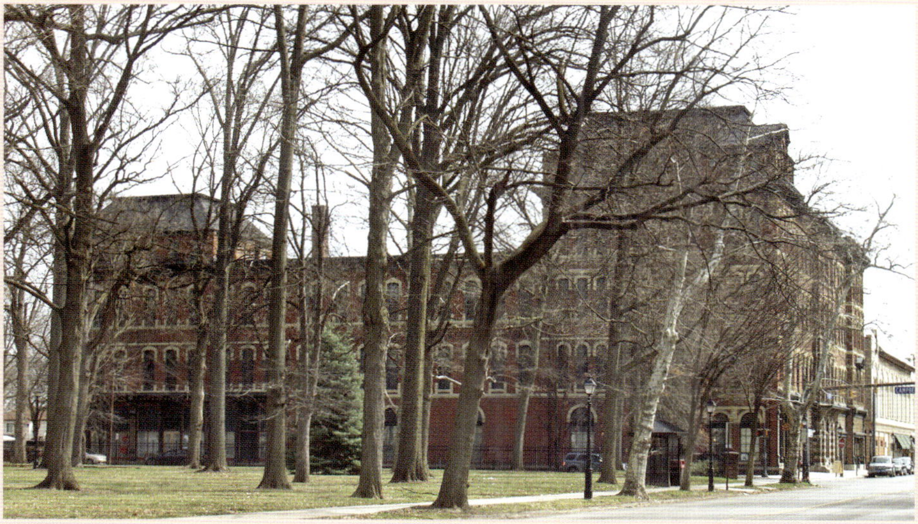

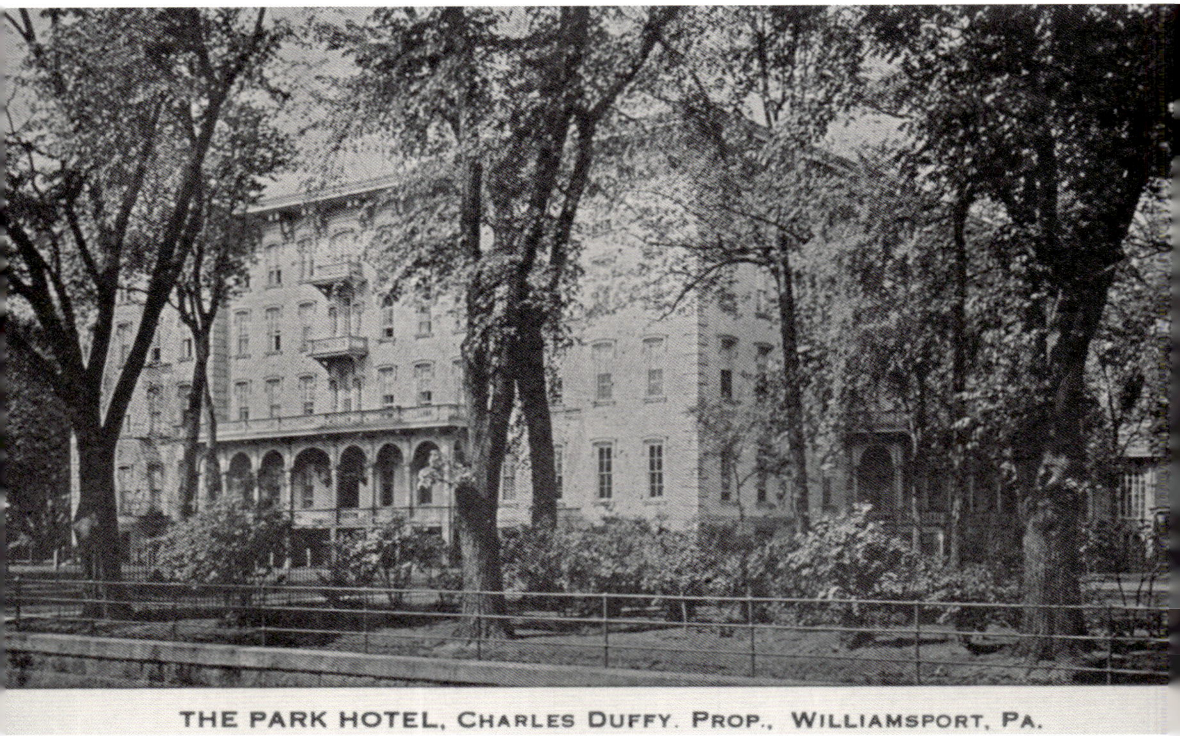

The Herdic House was built on the "Grove Lot" at West Fourth and Campbell Streets in 1865. Peter Herdic built the four-story hotel to facilitate the necessary relocation of the passenger depot on Pine Street. He conveyed the land for the new depot to the railway and agreed that he would build an accompanying hotel adjacent to it. Today, it is a two-story office building; however, much of its original exterior style remains.

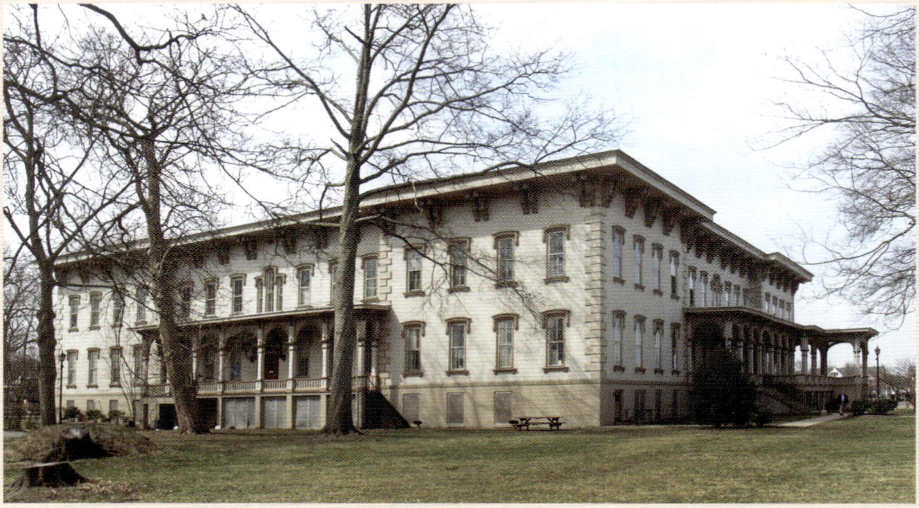

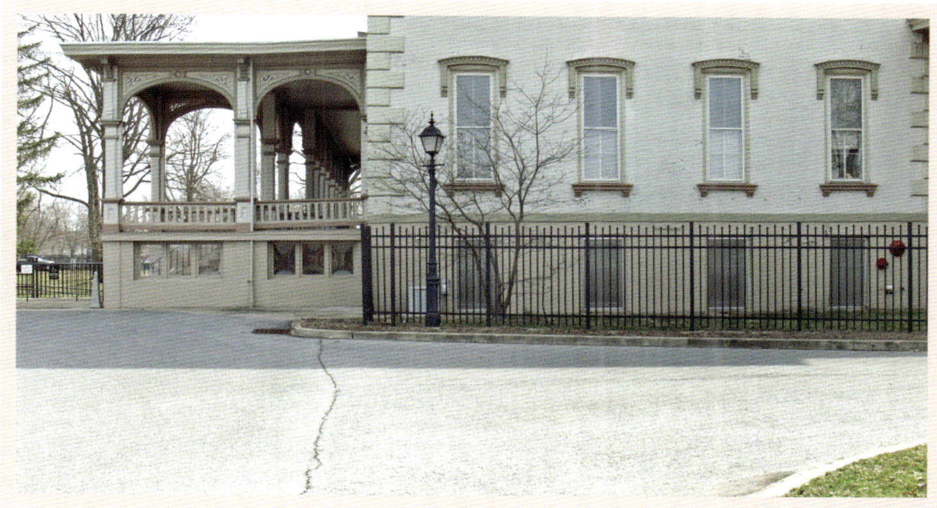

The name of the Herdic House was changed to Park Hotel in 1878 when Peter Herdic went bankrupt and was forced to sell the hotel at a great loss. As seen below behind the tourist bus, there was a restaurant with a bar and grill on the lowest level. In the 1930s, the hotel lost its top two stories when it was converted to a home for elderly women.

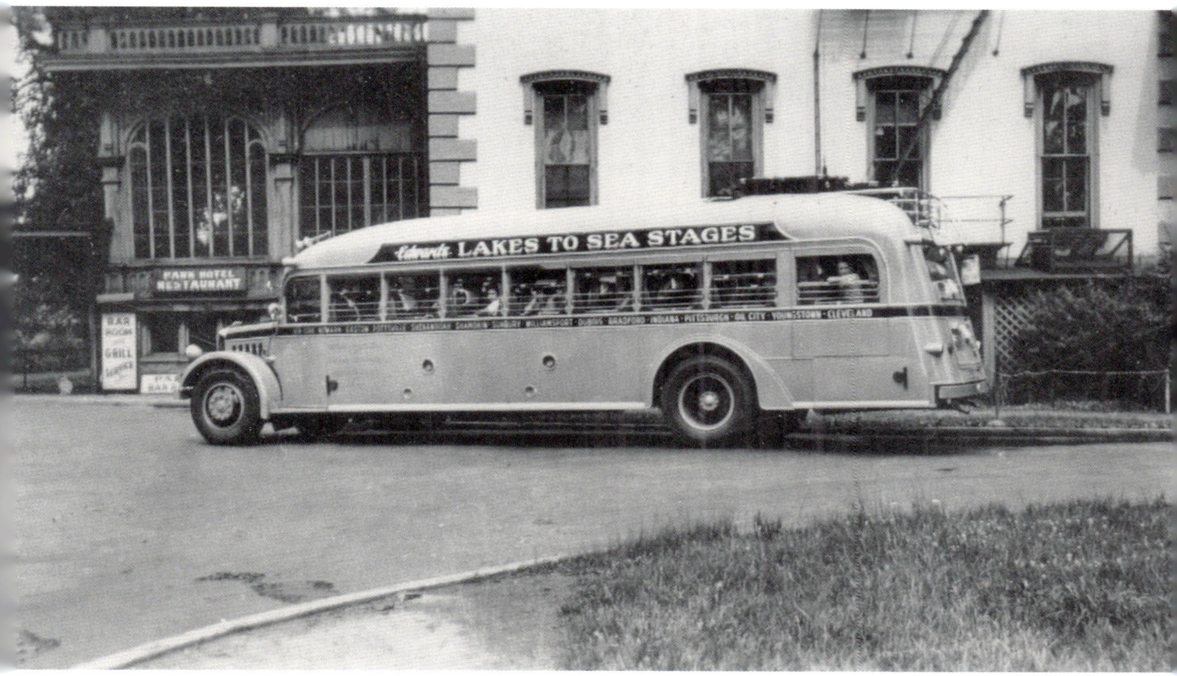

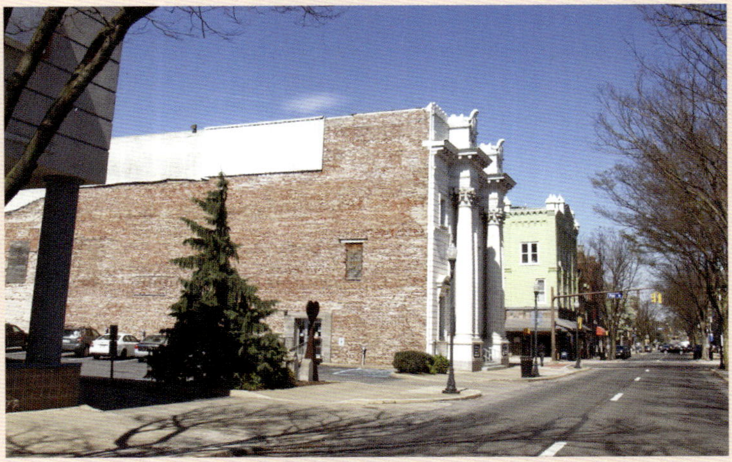

Looking east toward Pine Street, Lucius L. Walton's drugstore can be seen in the distance below. Today, it is home to Alabaster Coffee Roaster & Tea Company. Also of note is Reed, Muir & Co. featuring a large selection of postcards. That building is now a parking lot; however, the Reed, Muir & Co. seen in the vintage photograph eventually became C.A Reed Paper Products, a multimillion-dollar business that was sold to Westvaco in the late 1960s.

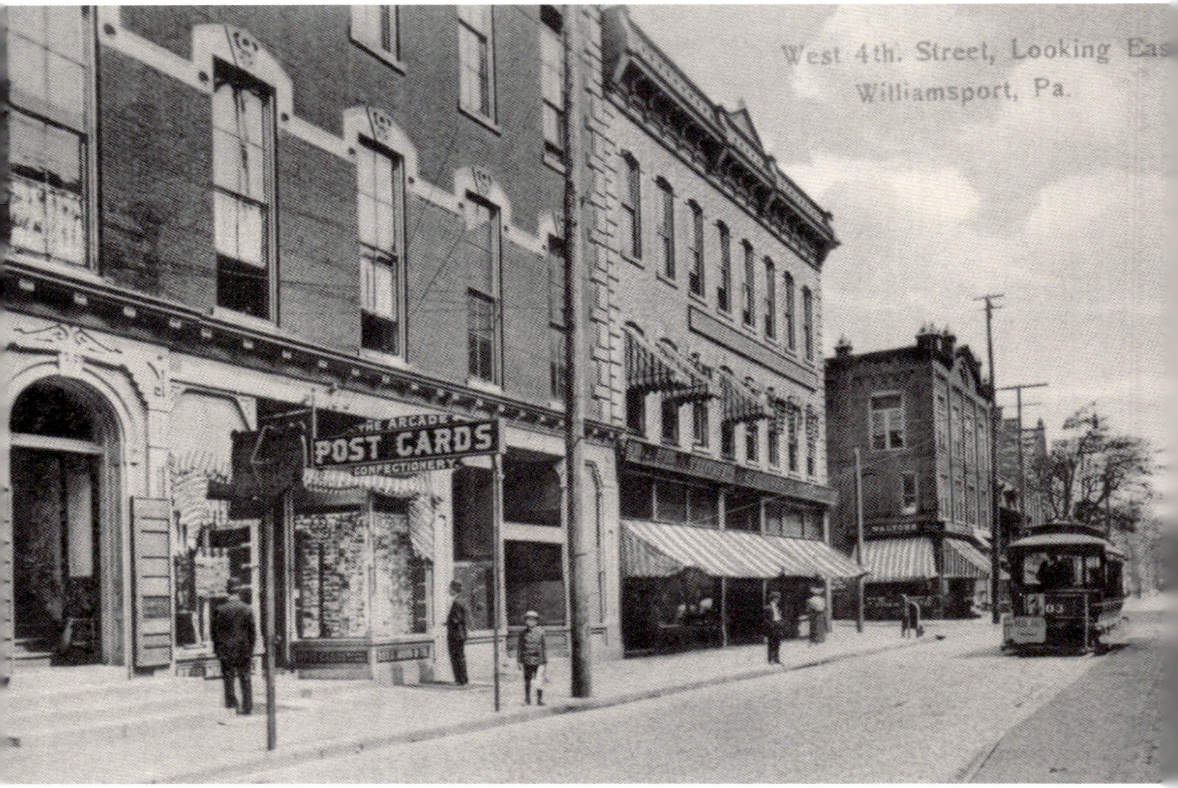

CHAPTER 4

Organizations and Public Places

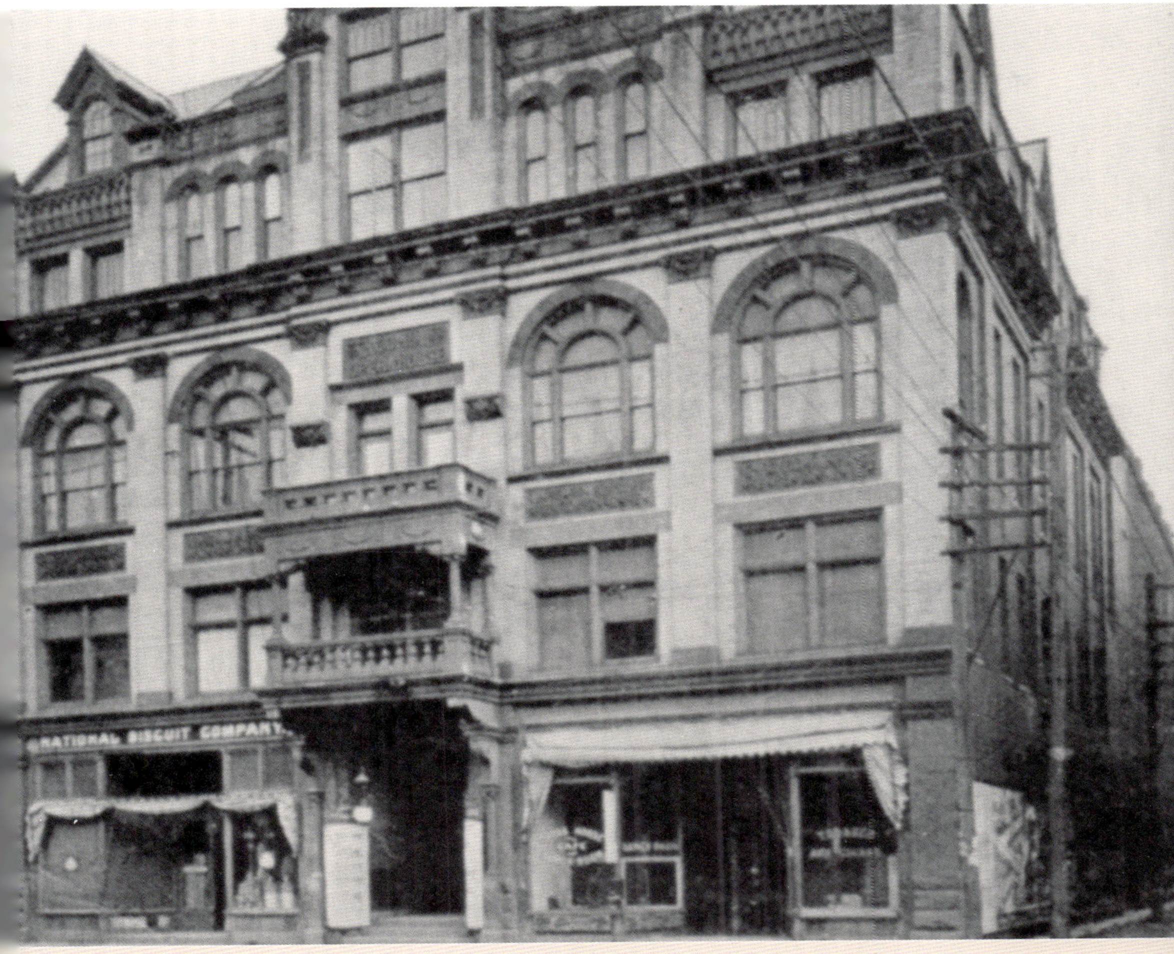

The Lycoming Opera House was dedicated on September 9, 1892. It was built with 1,800 seats and two balconies. It quickly became the theatrical center of the county, drawing the country's greatest stars. On the morning of May 31, 1915, the opera house and all its contents were lost to a fire. Today, a parking garage stands in its place.

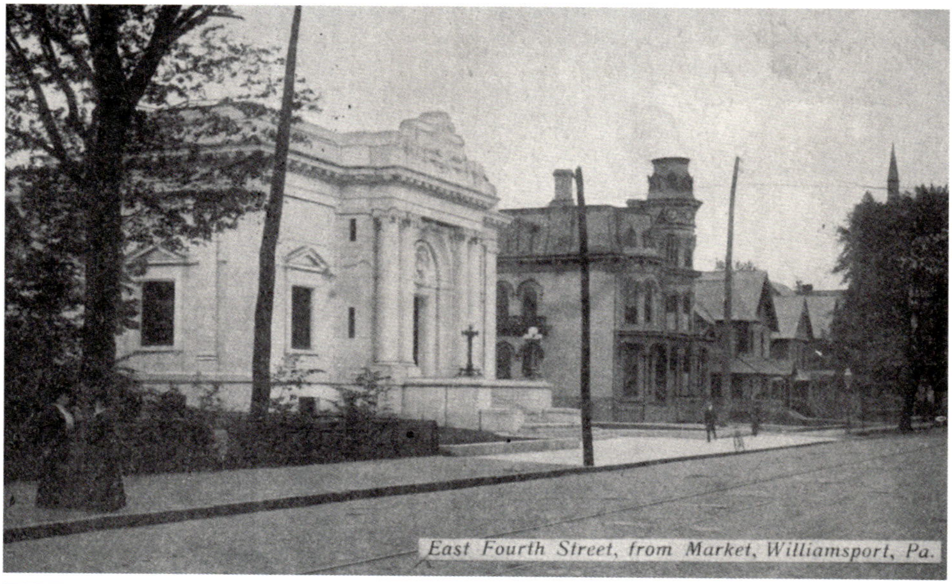

James V. Brown had a dream of a public library for the city. He hired architect Edgar V. Seeler and chose the location. Sadly, he died before he could see his ambition through. However, almost three years after his death, in June 1907, the James V. Brown Library opened, thanks to his generous bequest. Today, it serves the entire county with numerous services and programs. Over 500 print books a day are borrowed, along with many more digital and audiobooks.

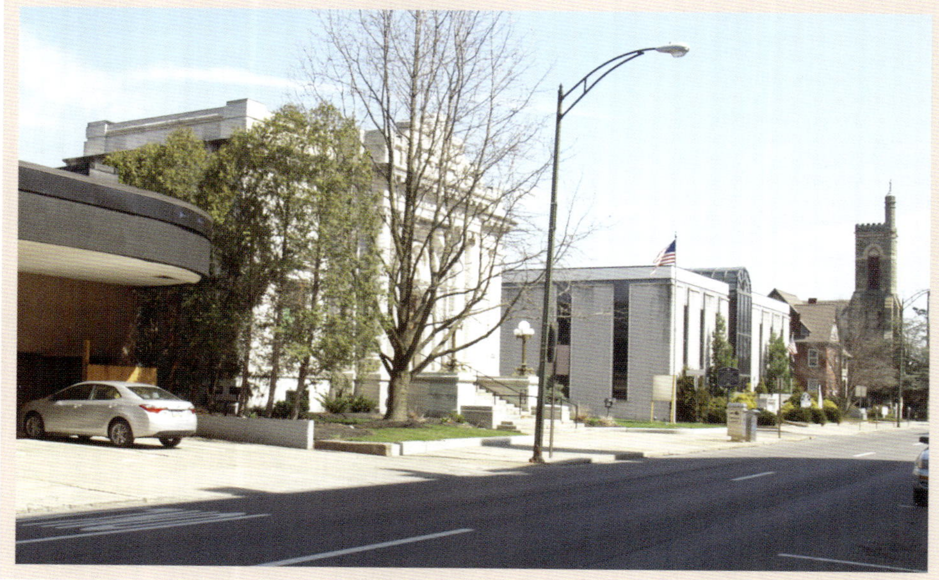

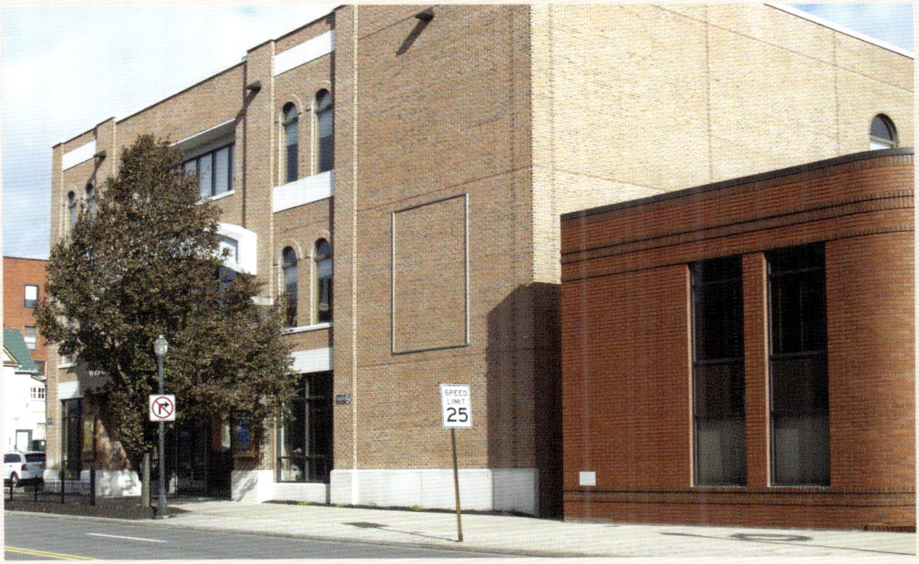

Dr. S.S. Koser and his wife, Dr. C. Williamsee Koser, erected the Koser Sanitarium in 1909. The first floor contained offices, storerooms, and at the time of the photograph below, Beck & Beck Laundrymen. Hospital rooms were above. The c. 1834 livery stables built with 12-by-12 hewn stocks of white pine were removed to make way for this private hospital. The Welch Children's Wing opened here in 2009 and was featured as a "Best in Library Design" by the American Library Association.

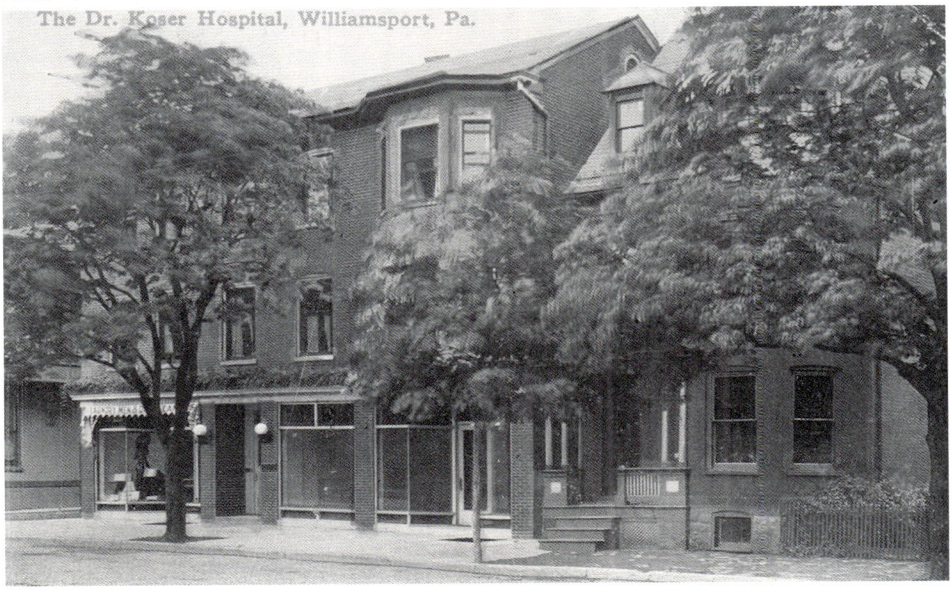

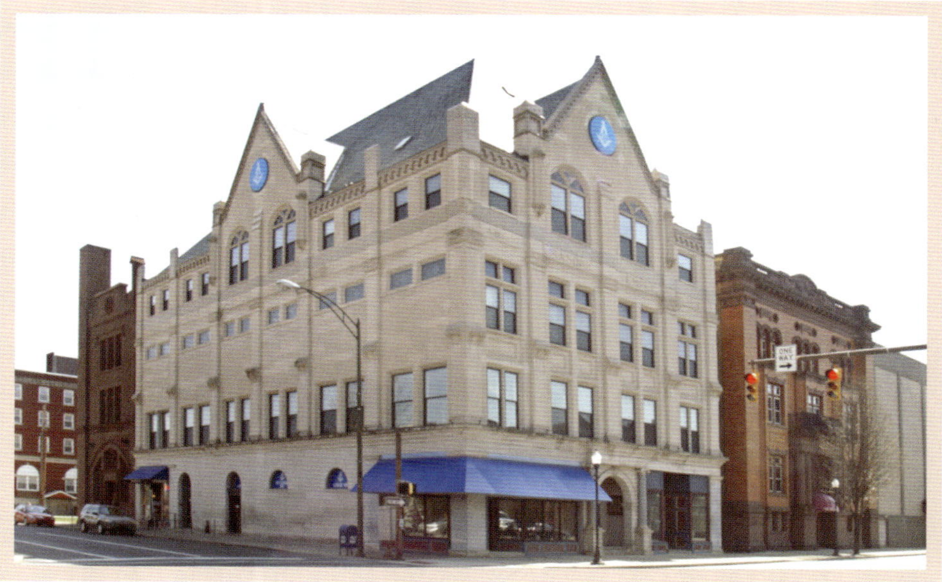

The Masonic temple was built in 1898 at the former site of the Second Presbyterian Church and is still there today. The Acacia Club is next to the Masonic temple, and to the right of it in the vintage photograph below is the Occidental Hotel. The old hotel was purchased in 1919 by the Scottish Rite Masons. Today, the Scottish Rite Auditorium sits where the hotel was and occupies an additional two lots.

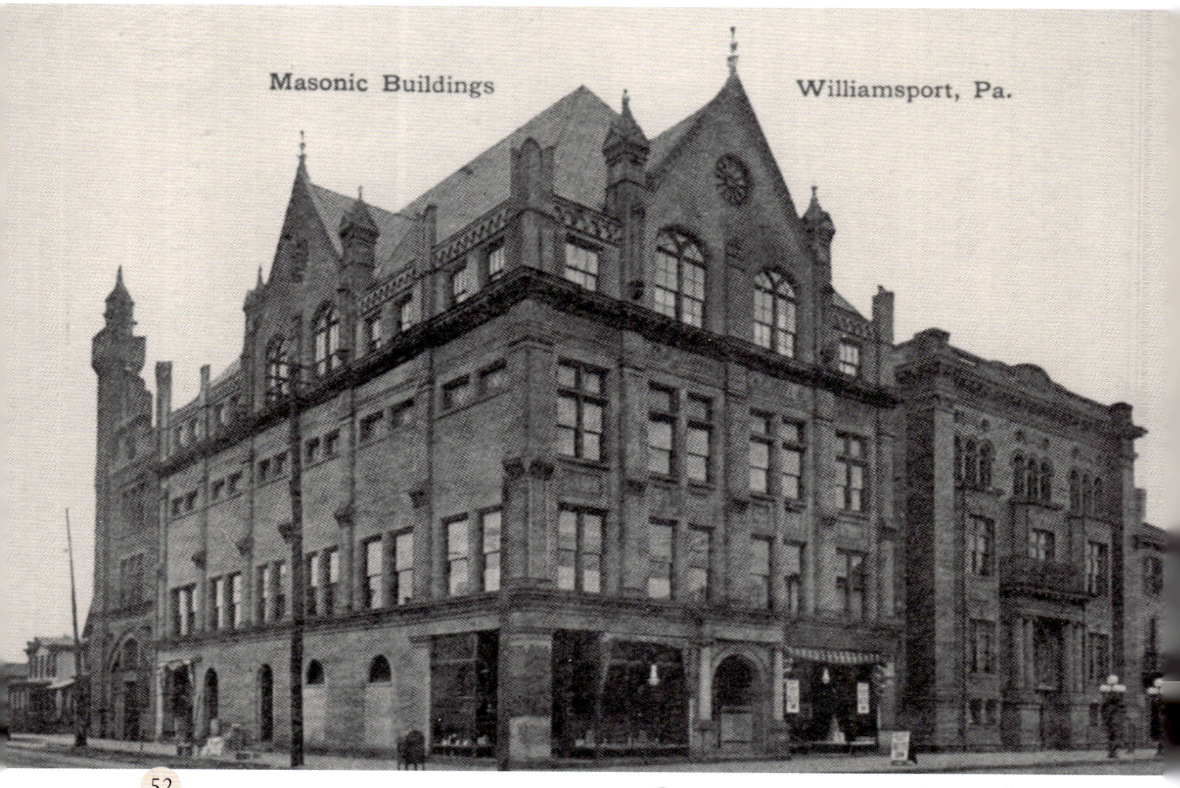

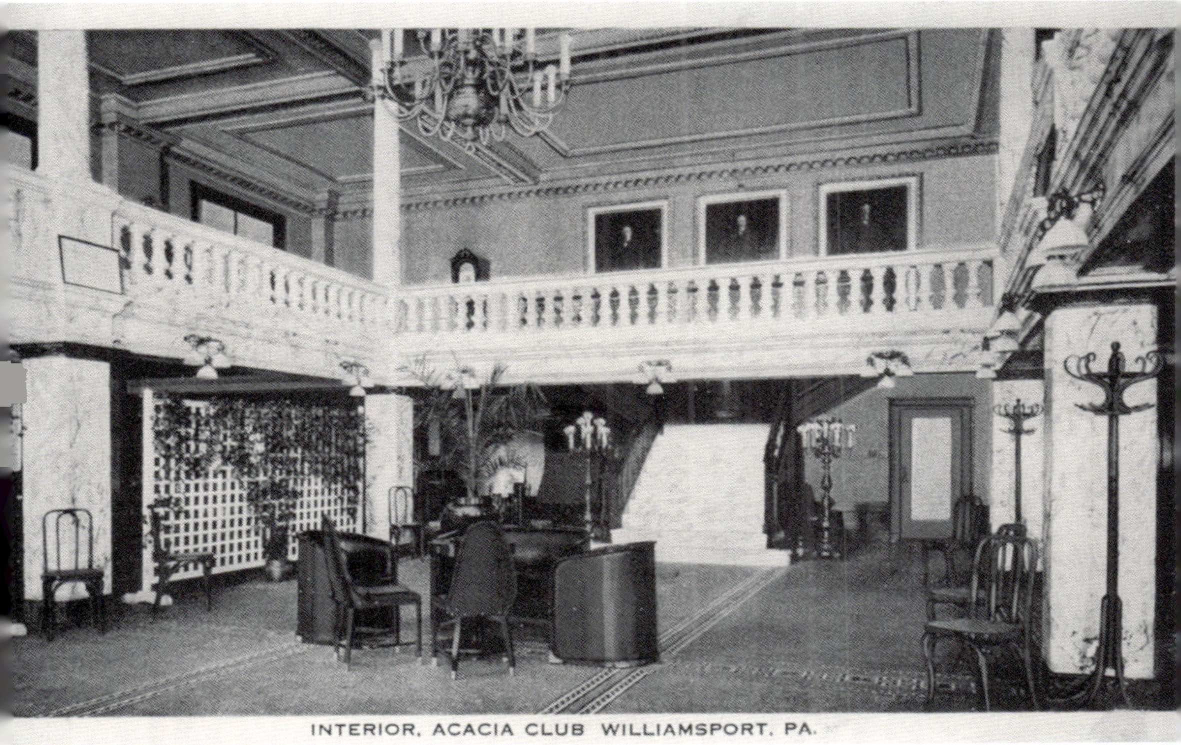

The Acacia Club was built in 1910 for the members of the Scottish Rite. Today, it is used by both the members and the public for parties and events. Even the furnishings have been preserved, including the grandfather clock to the left of the stairs on the mezzanine. The lamp stands flanking the bottom of the staircase are also original. The coat racks and the desk, which cannot be seen in the modern photograph, are currently elsewhere in the building.

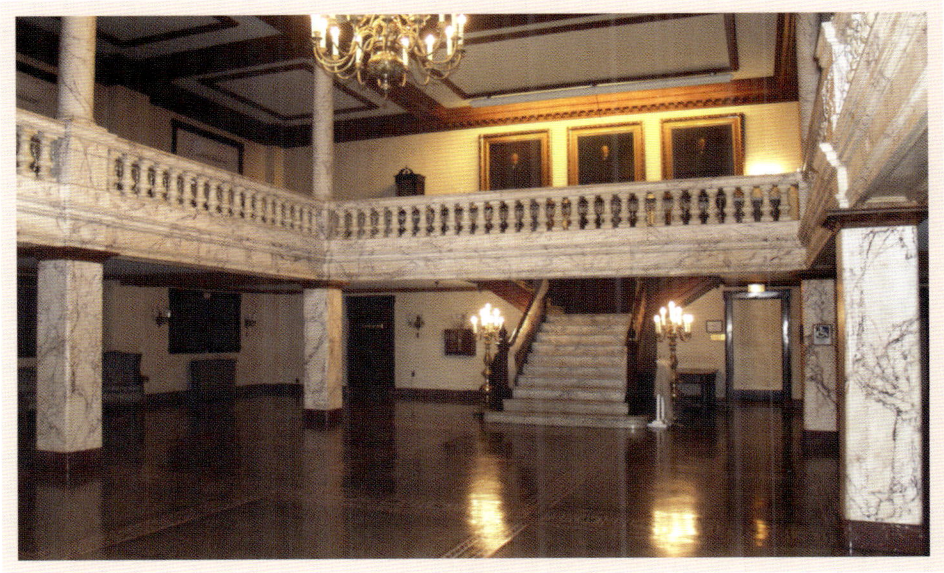

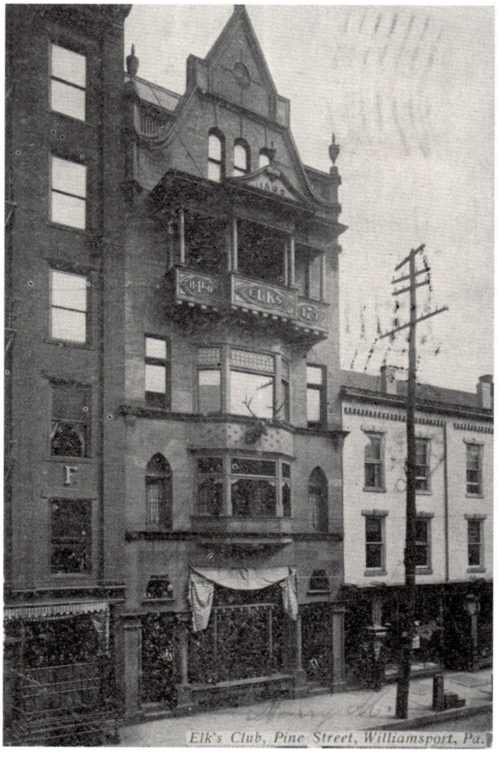

This building on Pine Street was the Elks Lodge 173 until the Elks moved to East Fourth Street in 1927. The building to the right of it was Casper's pool hall at the time of the vintage photograph, sometime before 1906. That building survived until a large fire in 1980 took it and nine other businesses. Today, the Lycoming County Executive Plaza is where this commercial block once was.

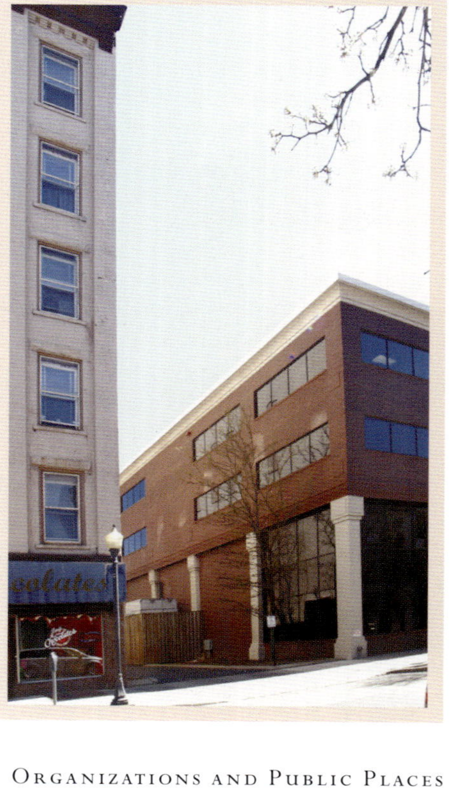

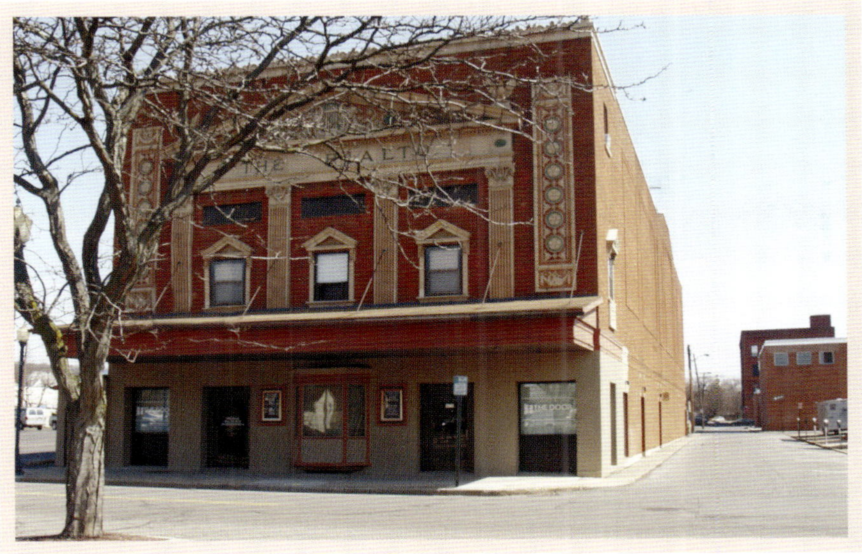

This 1850s house at 470 Pine Street had been a boardinghouse, a private school for girls, a YWCA, and the Fraternal Order of Eagles. In 1927, the Rialto Theater was built on this site. In 1980, the theater, much in need of attention, was purchased by the Door Fellcwship Church. The church renovated it, keeping its historical look both inside and out.

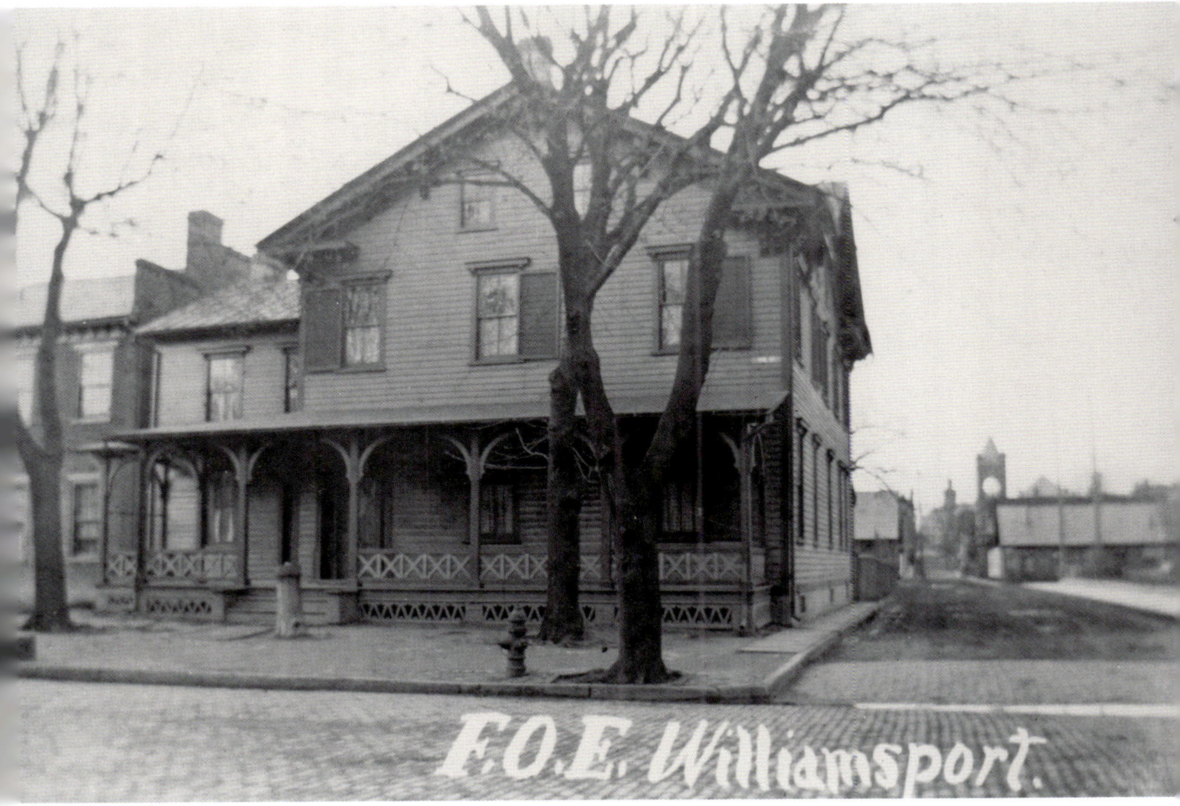

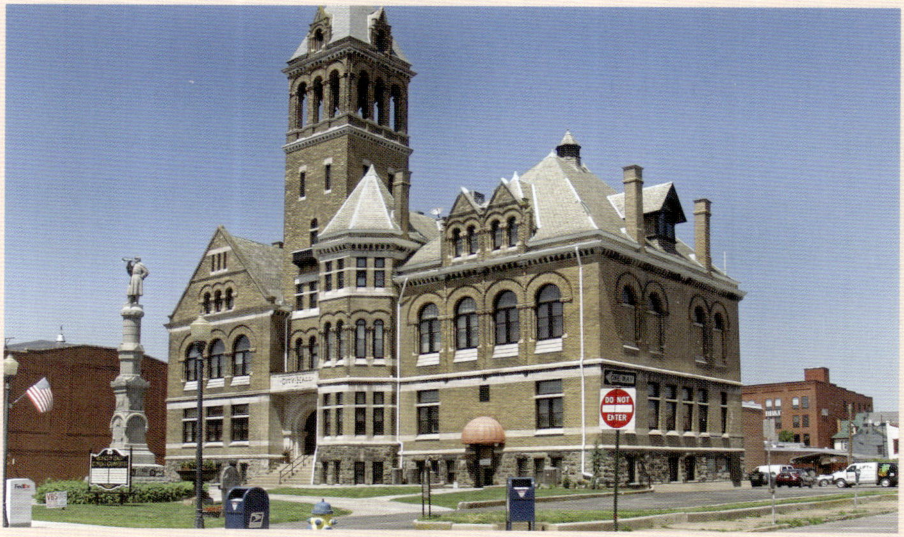

City hall's cornerstone was laid on July 4, 1893, and one year later, the dedication ceremony was held. The Sailors and Soldiers Monument was placed in front of the new city hall around the same time, but its location was controversial. According to newspaper reports, most citizens, including Mayor Elliot, preferred it to be placed in Brandon Park, but the committee voted for the present spot. The monument is still there, but this building is no longer city hall (see page 57).

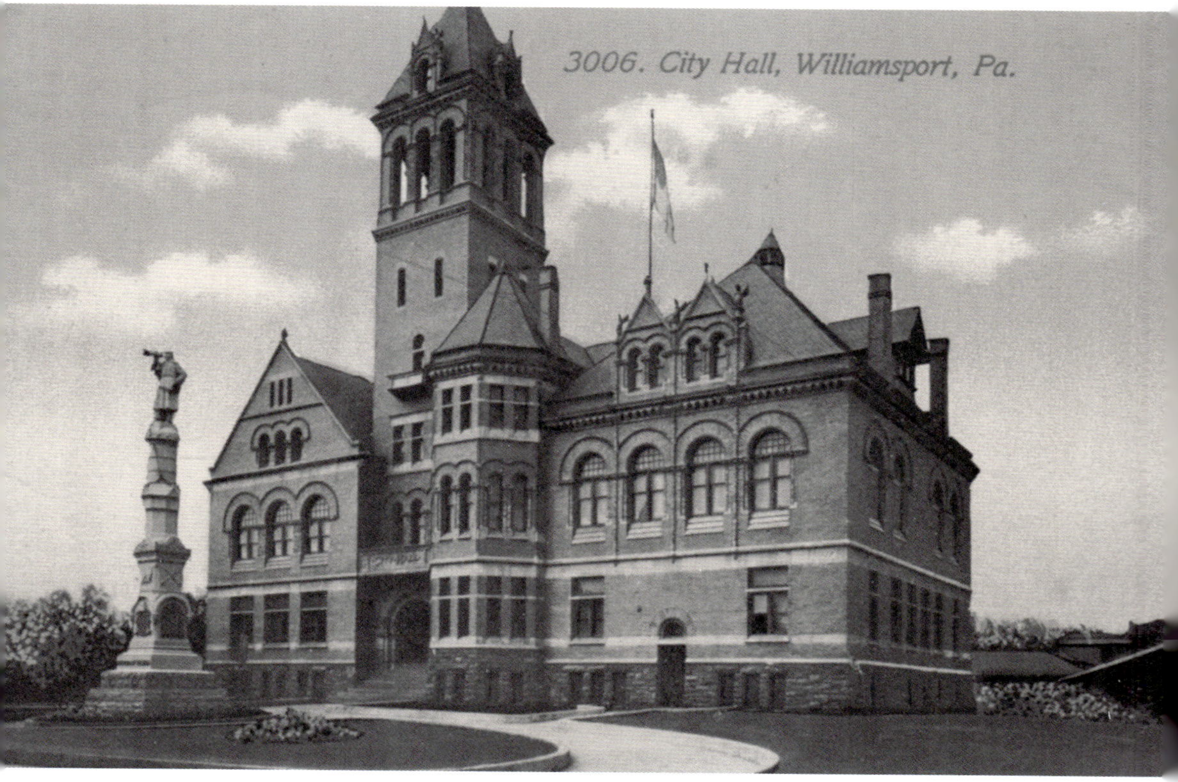

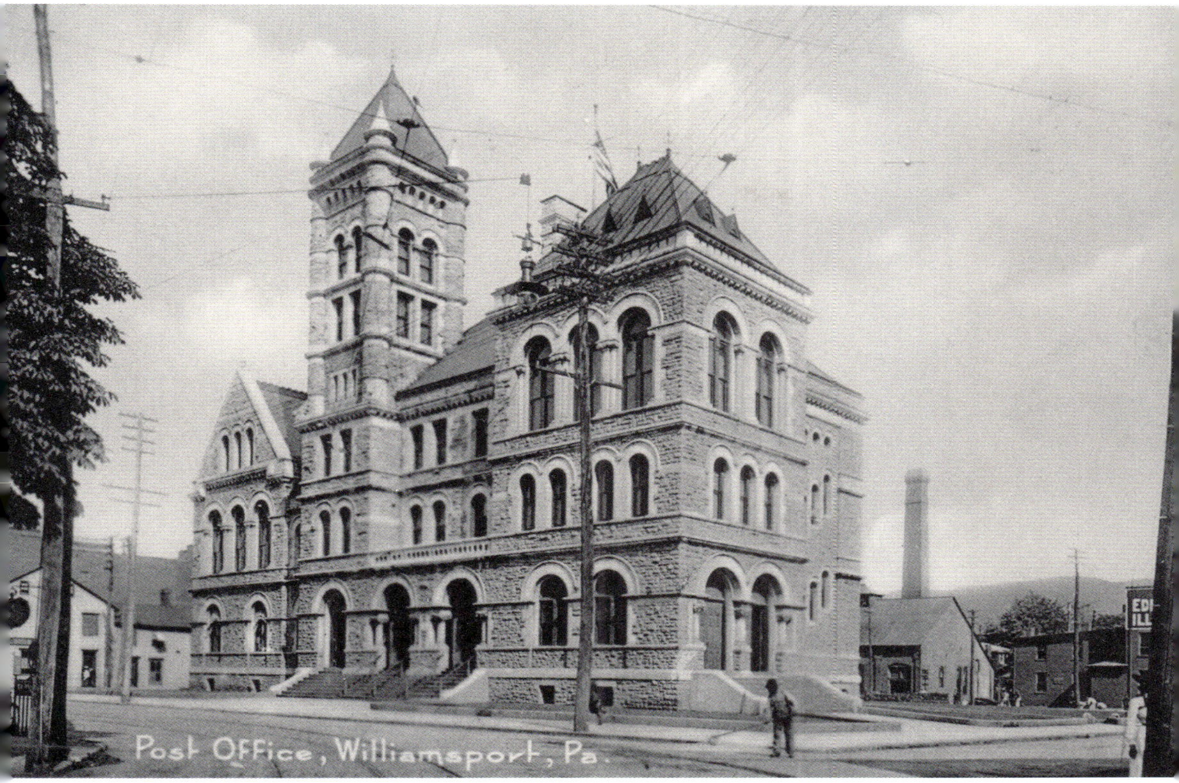

This building that is currently city hall opened in 1891 as a federal building with a post office on the first floor and courtrooms and offices above. Today, the structure remains largely unaltered from its original exterior, except for an addition behind it, which was carefully planned to match the older portion. Inside, the original post office bays are partially covered but can still be seen, and many interior architectural elements have been left original.

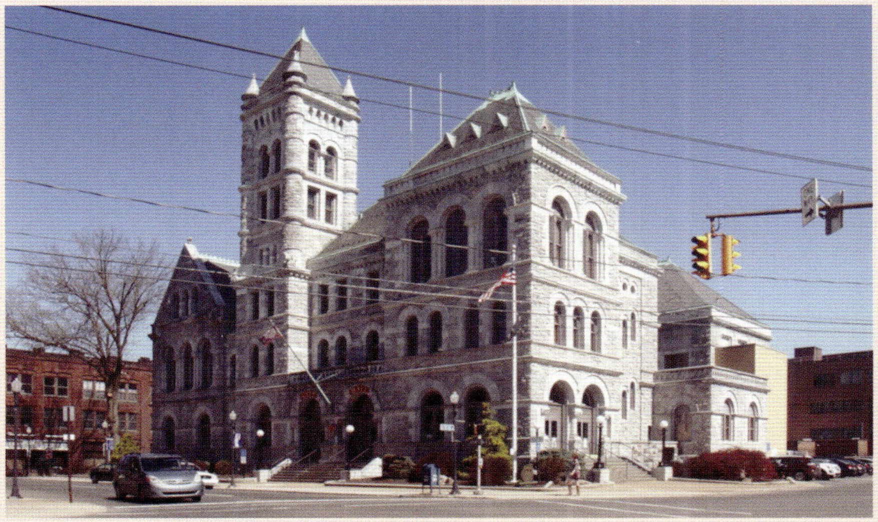

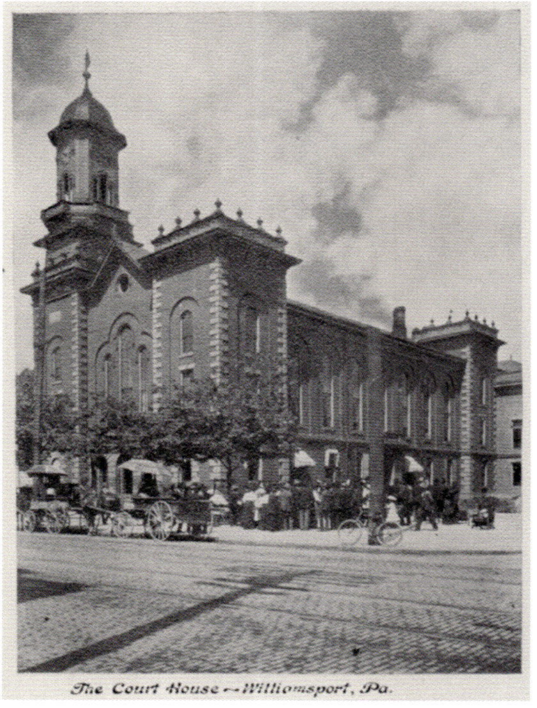

Auctions, like the one seen in the vintage photograph at left, were regular events on the pavement at the old county courthouse. Local business owners complained about them because of the mess they made, so in 1909, a resolution was passed to end them. It was, however, decided that the woman who had the candy stand on the corner could remain because it was her only means of livelihood. The 1860 courthouse was demolished in 1969 to build the larger one seen below.

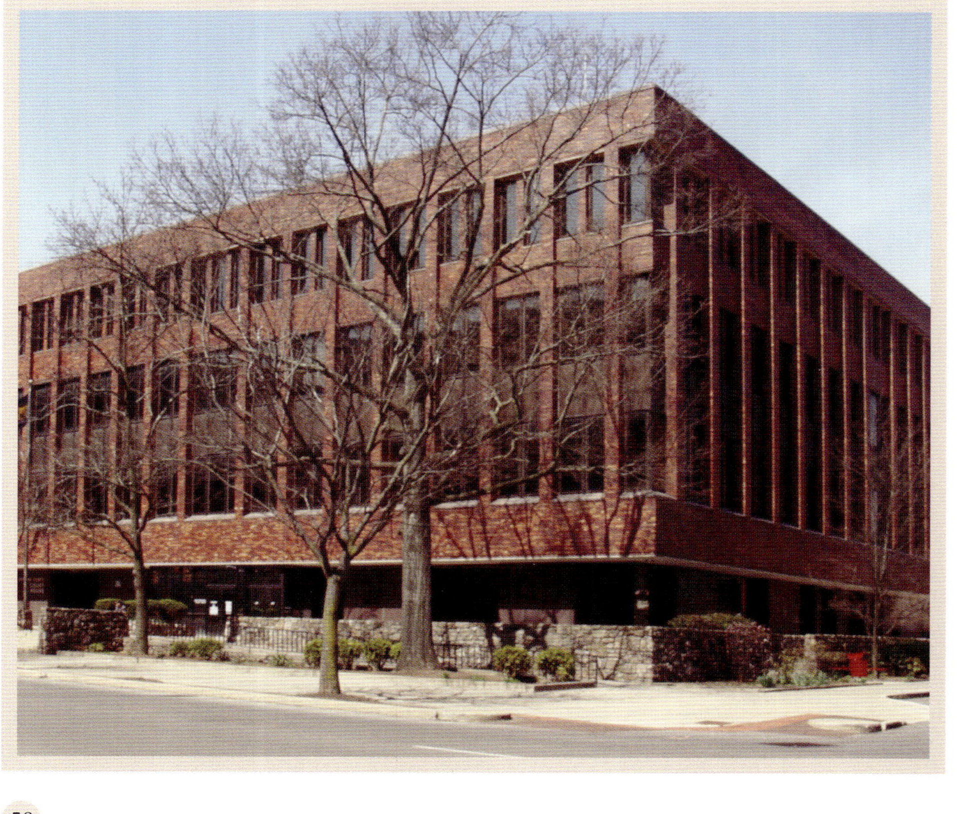

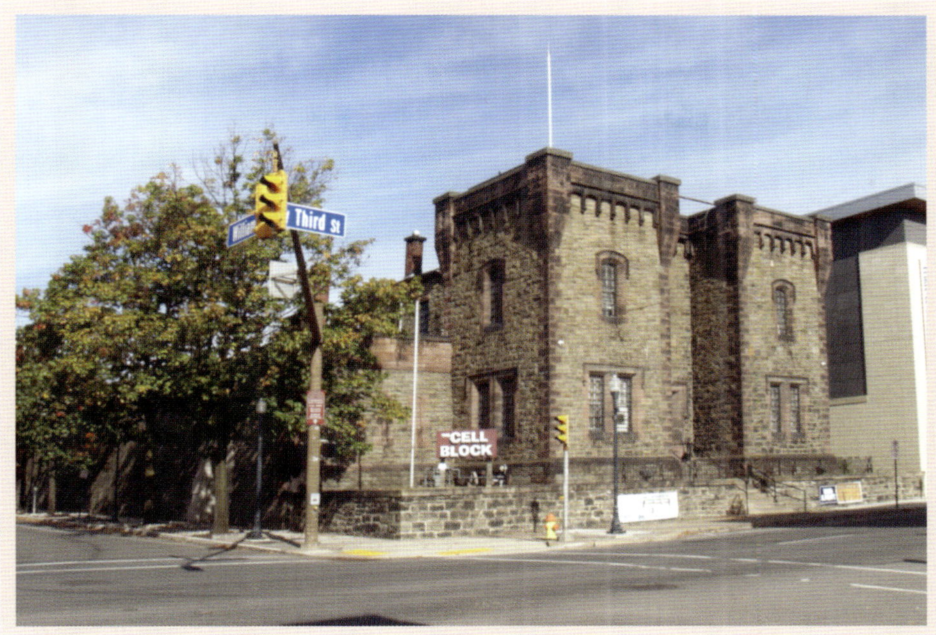

The jail shown here was built in 1868 on the site of an older, c. 1799 jail. Originally, it had a tower with a bell that rang after each hanging. The widely unpopular decision to remove it in the late 1920s was reportedly due to lack of use and irreparable damage, though it was claimed by some that it could have been repaired. In 1986, a new prison opened, and today, the old jail is a popular nightclub.

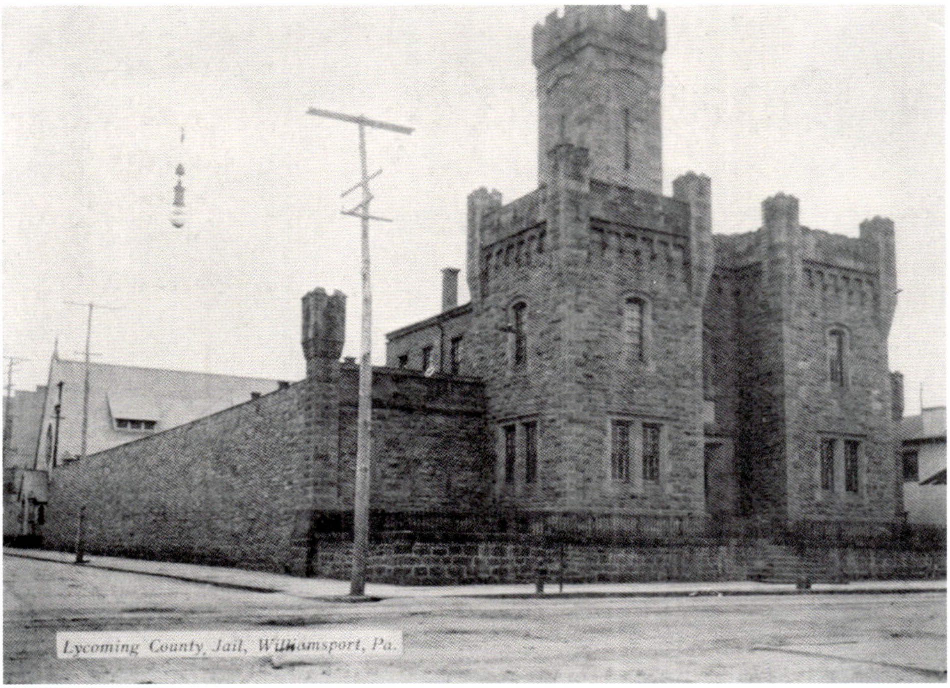

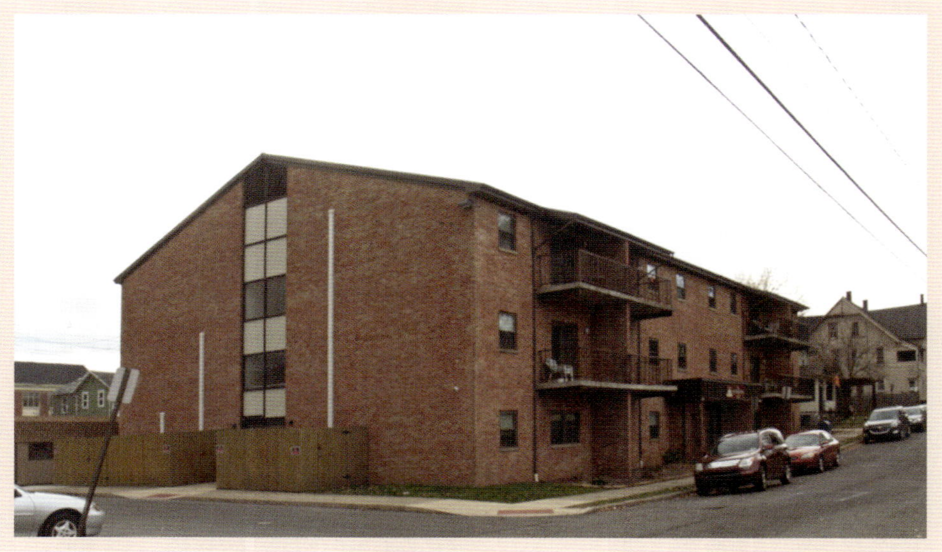

Mary Slaughter was a former slave and the founder of the Home for Aged Colored Women. Originally run from a house on Walnut Street, she moved it to this site on Brandon Place in 1899. It continued for another 74 years until the building could not meet state standards for nursing homes. It was torn down and replaced with the Mary Slaughter apartments, which were built to meet the housing needs of Lycoming County residents.

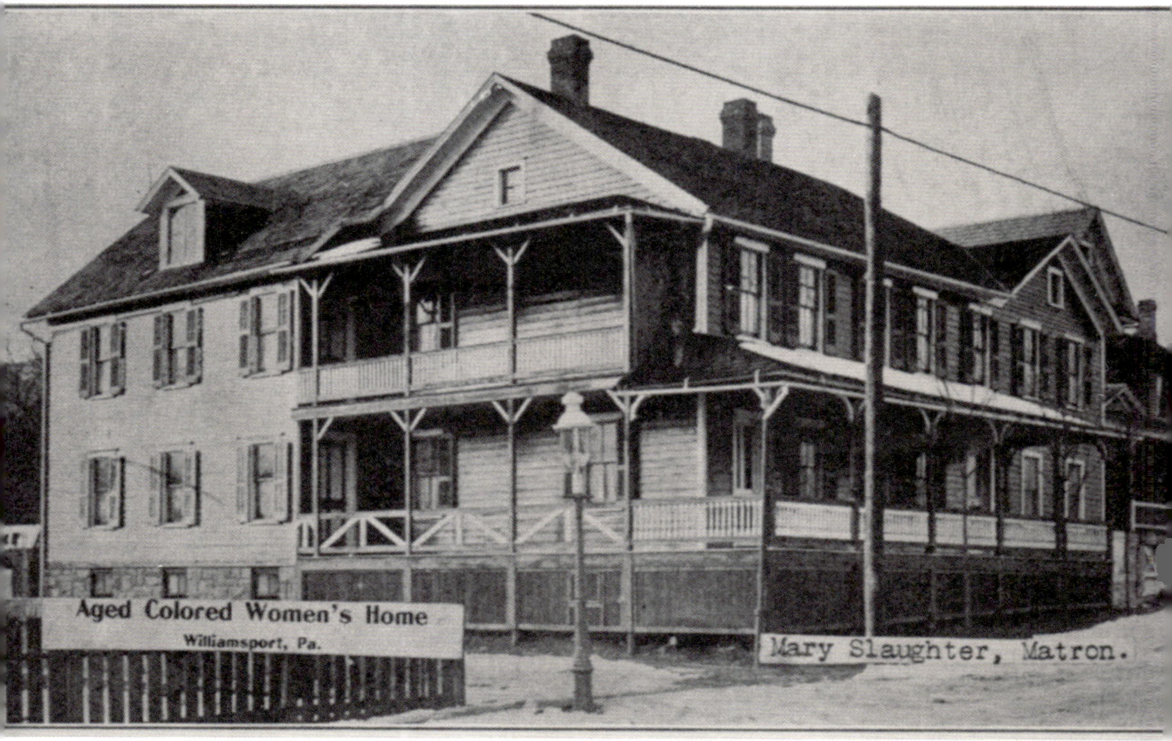

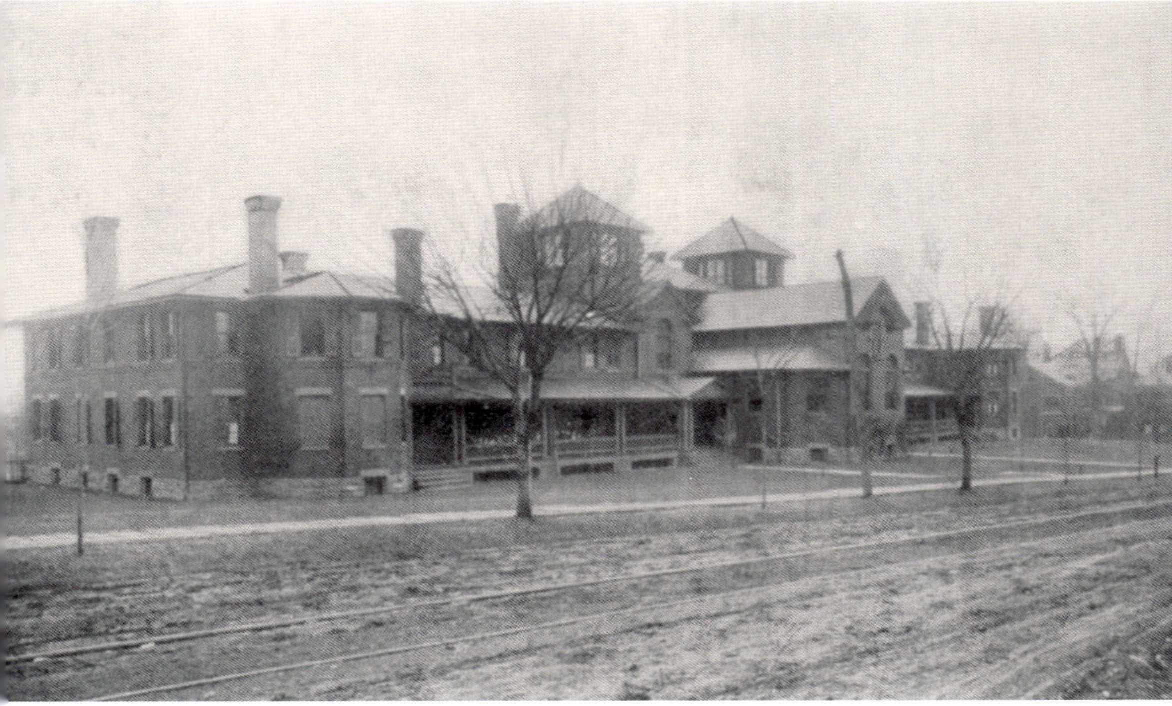

This was the Home for the Friendless, built in 1898 to provide for the care of children and elderly women. Originally, the ends of the building were square. The octagonal wings were added in the 1920s. The women were housed on the south side, with the children on the north side. The home has since relocated to Ravine Road, becoming a retirement community, and renamed the Williamsport Home. The former building is now used for doctors' offices.

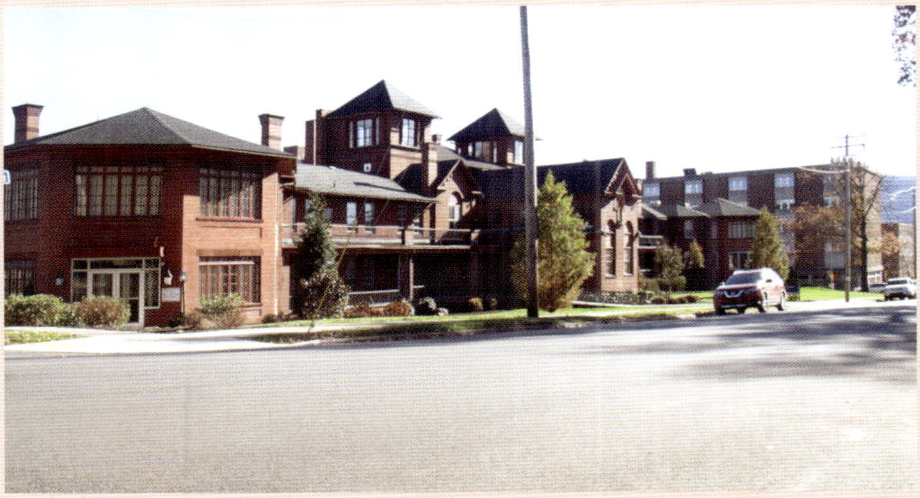

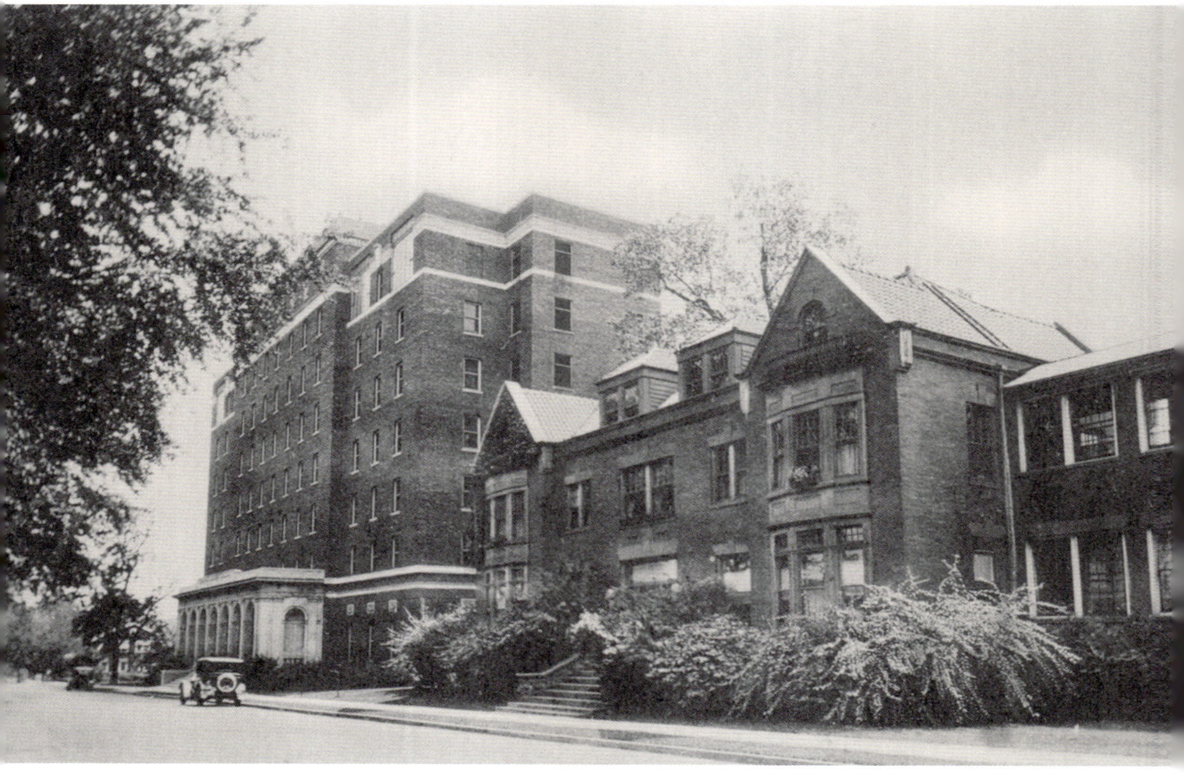

The Williamsport Hospital was built in 1891 on the site of Old Oaks Park. In the 1880s, the 27-acre park was popular for picnics and hosted many horse races. It had a half-mile oval racing track, ticket office, and grandstand that held 2,000 people. When the park was sold and broken up for building lots, the hospital purchased an entire block for its new building. The hospital is still there, though greatly expanded, and is now UPMC Susquehanna.

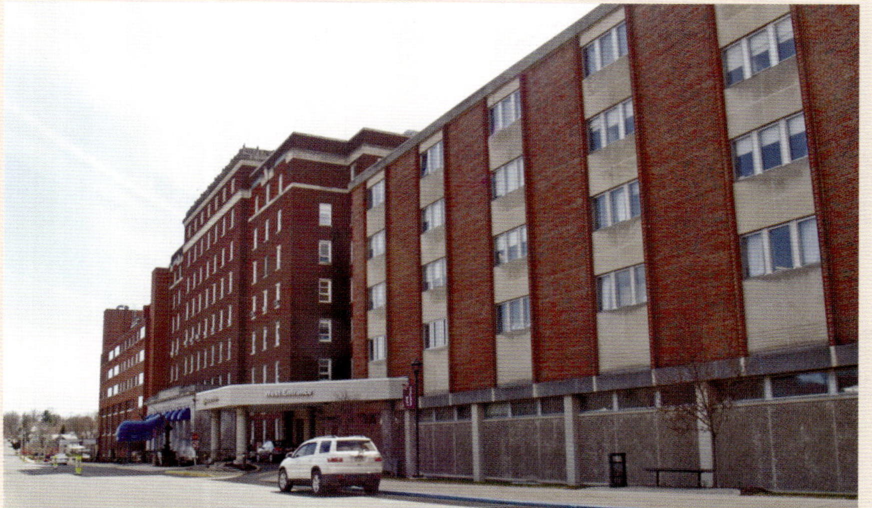

The YMCA, seen at center in the vintage photograph below, built its Williamsport location with a sizable stone arch doorway for the entrance. It opened in 1888 with social rooms, a library, reading rooms, a kitchen, storerooms, and gymnasium. In 1902, the gymnasium was enlarged and an auditorium was added. The YMCA moved, and the Knights of Columbus located here in the 1920s. Today, the building is gone, and a more modern one has replaced it.

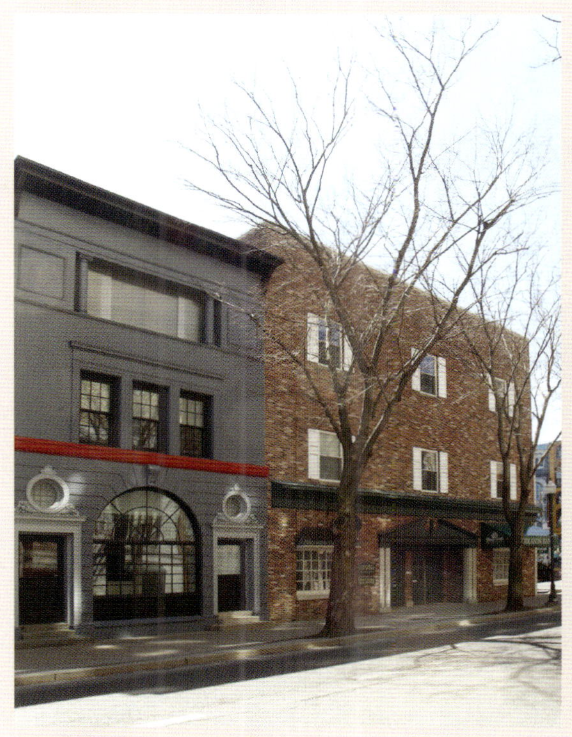

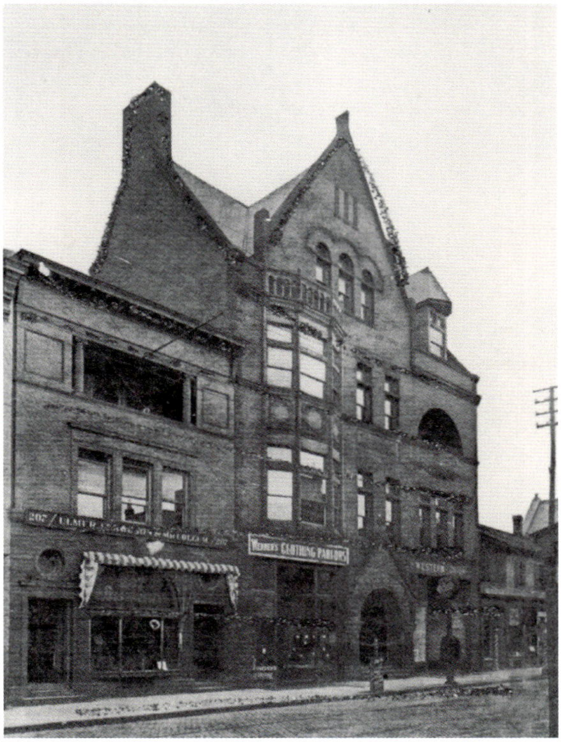

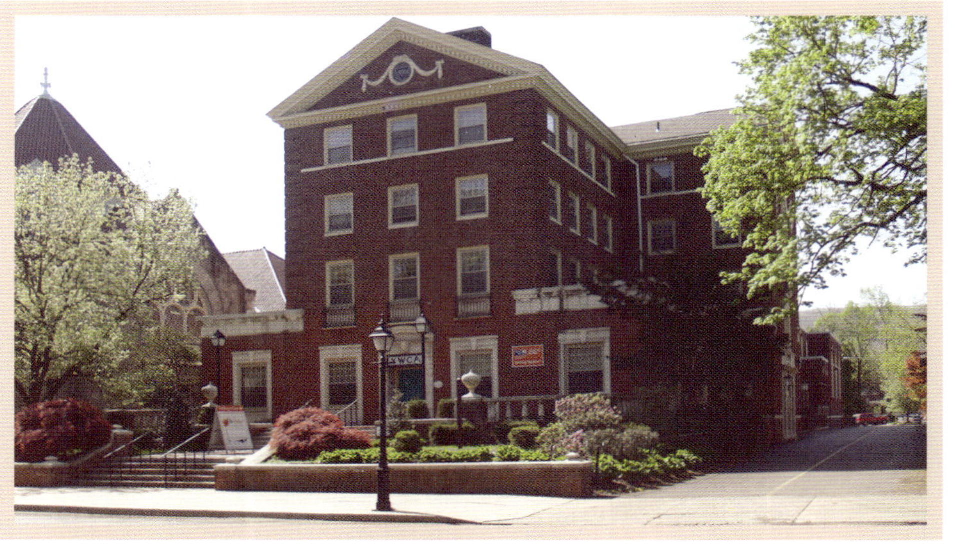

This building at 815 West Fourth Street was the first facility constructed as a YWCA in Williamsport. Previous YWCA buildings had been converted from other uses. It opened in 1929 as a combination residence and administration building with rooms for over 60 girls. There were club rooms and classrooms, a gymnasium, and a warm-water swimming pool. Today, the YWCA continues to serve the community from this building, which remains unchanged inside and out, though the swimming pool is no longer functional.

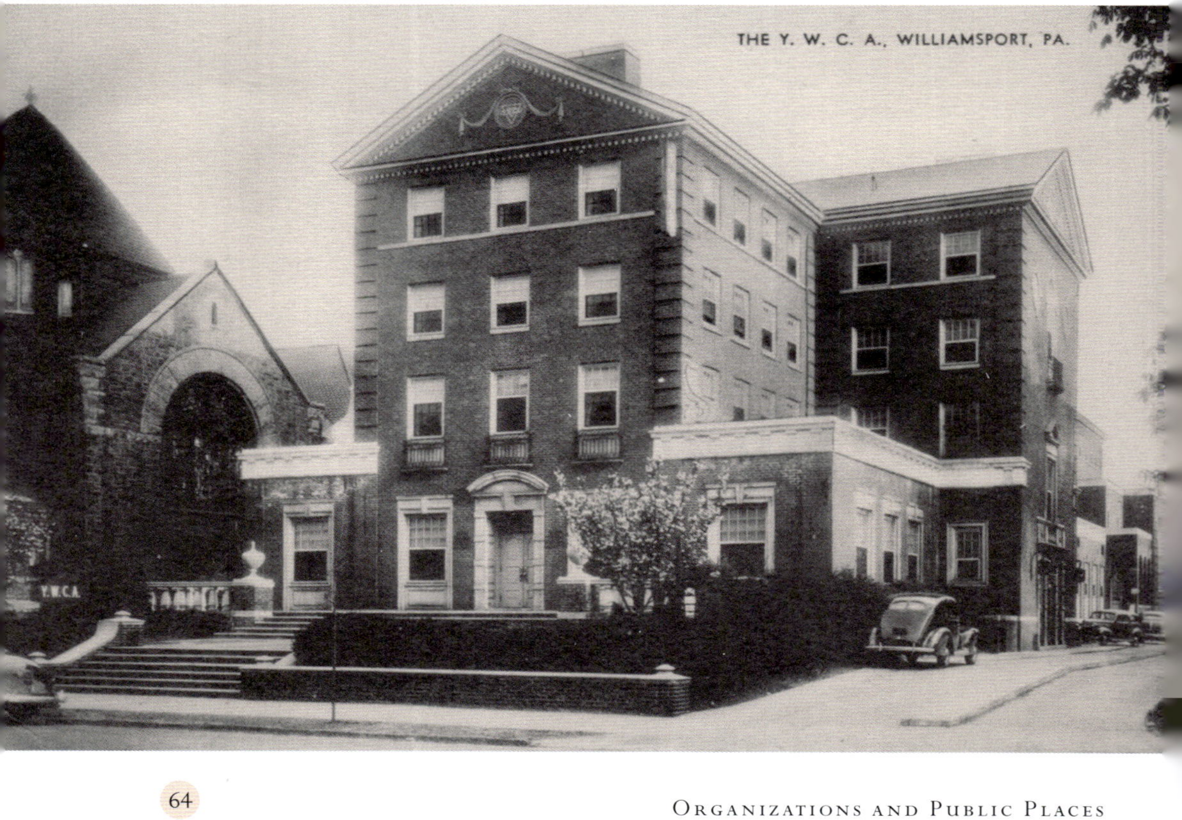

CHAPTER 5

CHURCHES

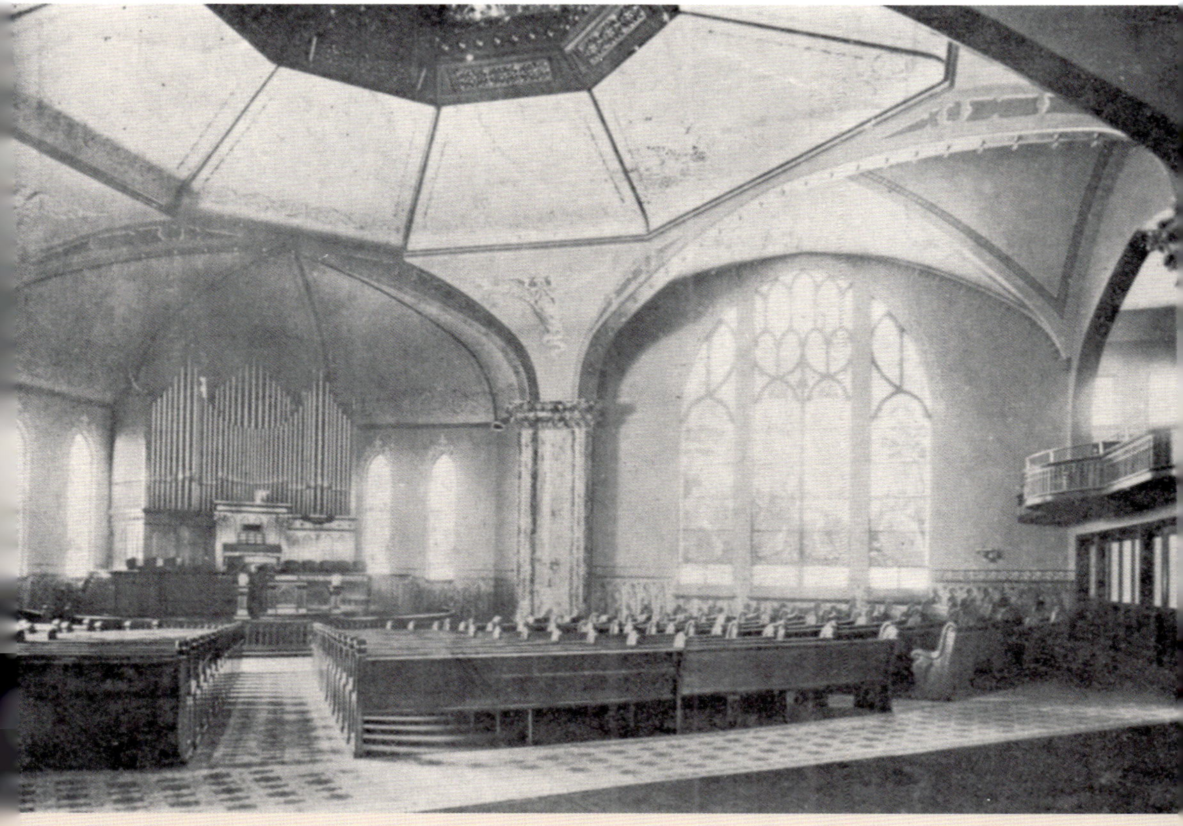

The interior of Pine Street Methodist Church is seen here shortly after its dedication on January 23, 1910. The rooms of the church, including the auditorium, Sunday school room, and galleries, had a seating capacity of 2,500. It was used regularly for services, lectures, concerts, and sermons. It was replaced by the current Pine Street Methodist Church in 1980.

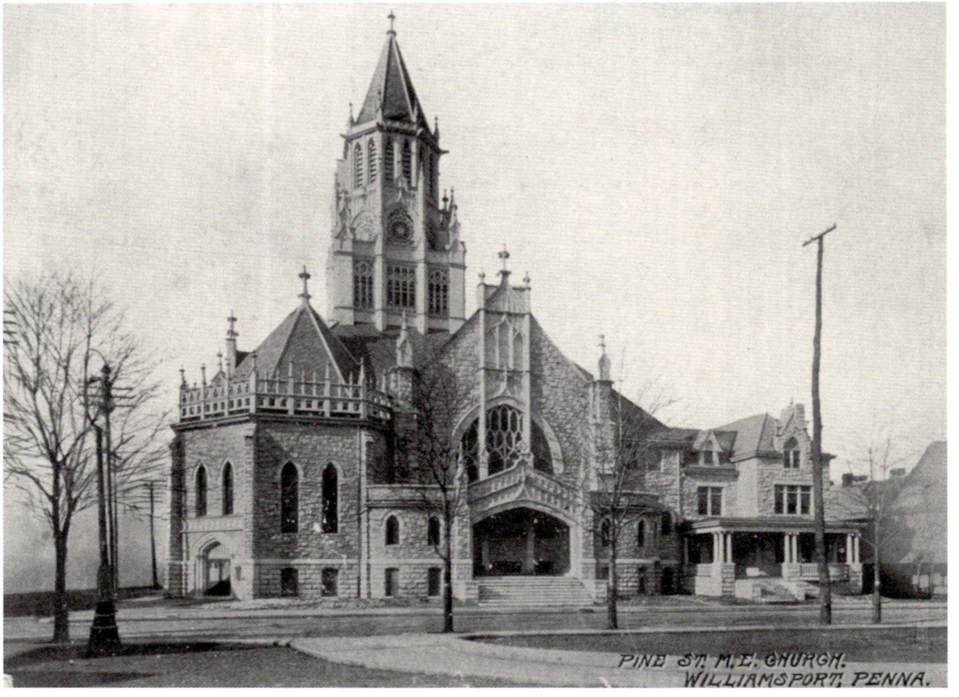

A previous Pine Street Methodist Church before the one shown above was built in 1844 and enlarged in 1869. The parsonage was built in 1864. By 1910, the church sought to accommodate the growing congregation, so the church shown in the vintage photograph was built on the same site. A fire destroyed it in 1977. The current church was completed in 1980. A further expansion was done in 1991; today, it encompasses an entire block.

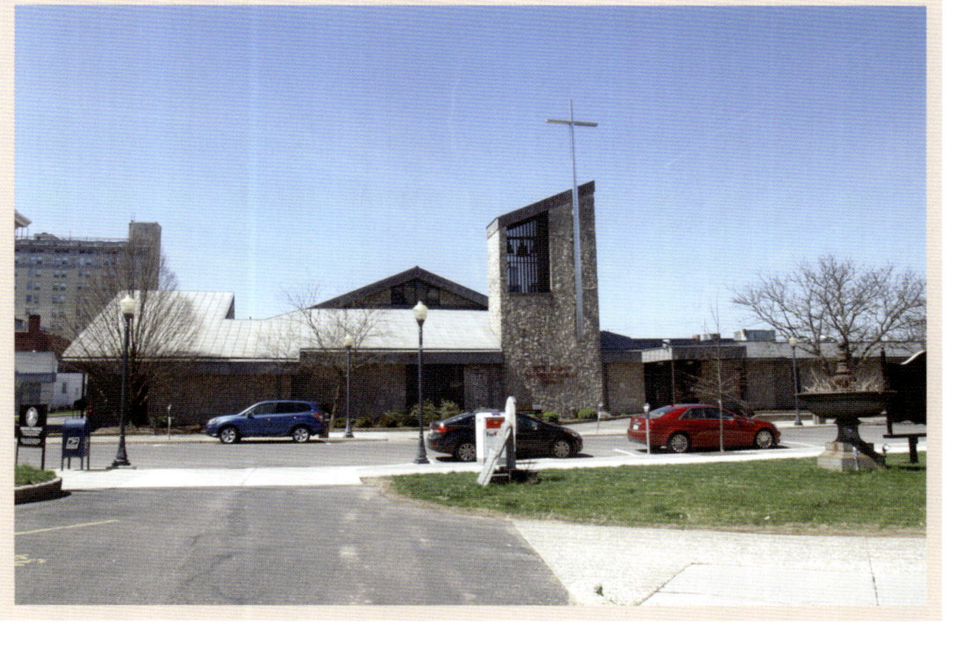

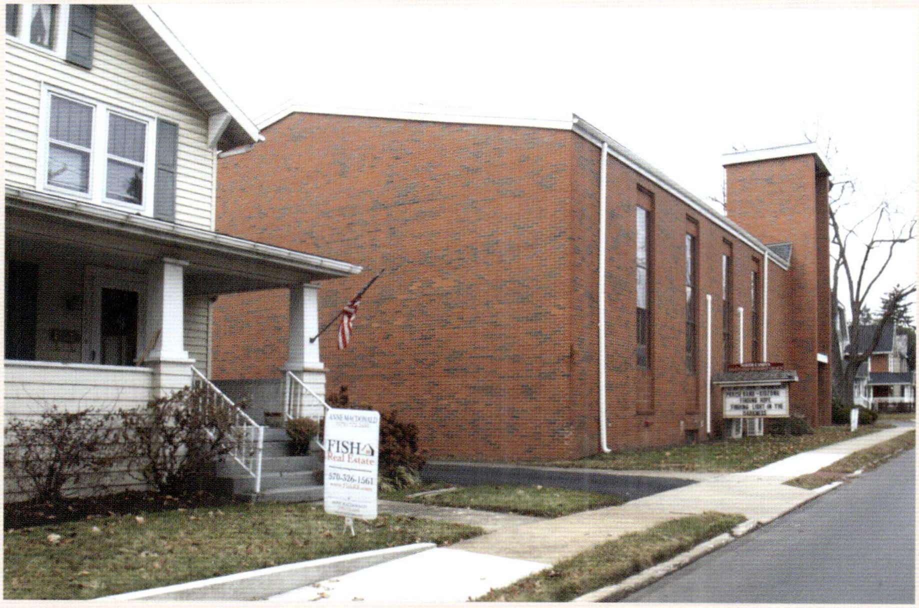

The Market Street Methodist Episcopal Church and parsonage were on the corner of Market and Belmont Streets. The lot for the parsonage was purchased in 1902 by the church but the parsonage, seen only in the vintage image, is no longer there. It stood where the church extends today. Interestingly, there is an existing twin to the parsonage just a few houses away. Presently, this church is now the North Campus of First Church United Methodist.

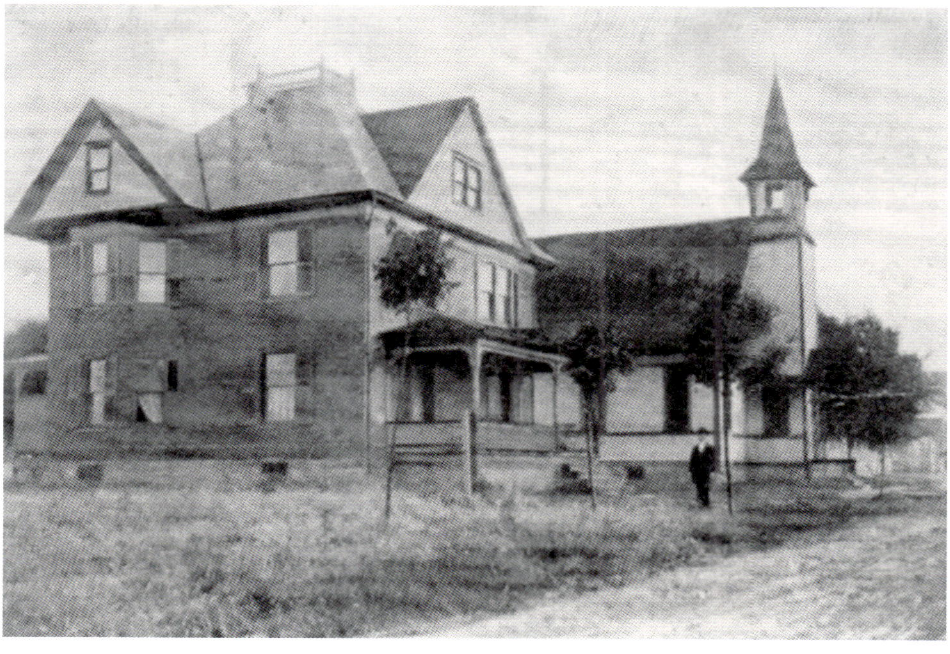

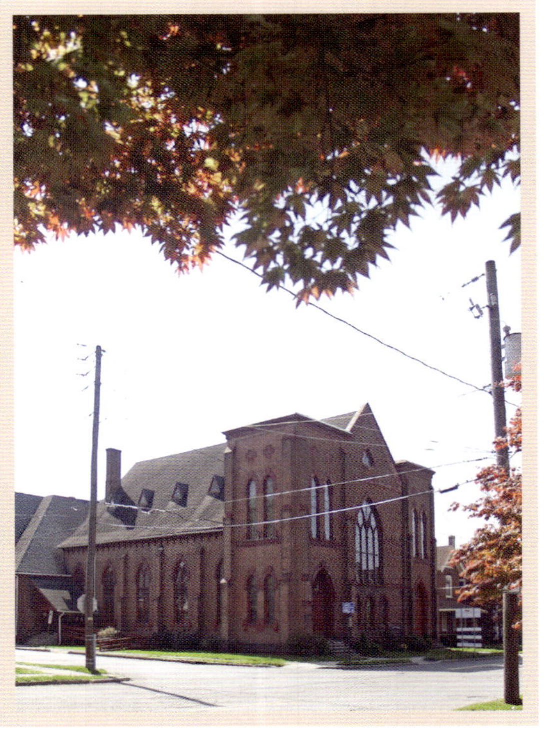

Built in 1880, the Grace Methodist Episcopal Church on Campbell Street originally had a 150-foot steeple. The church was furnished with a Gothic style pulpit and chairs in black walnut with maroon plush seats. The pew cushions were also maroon and stuffed with hair. The annex was added in 1888. Today, it is the American Rescue Workers' Saving Grace Shelter, which provides emergency shelter for families and individuals in crises.

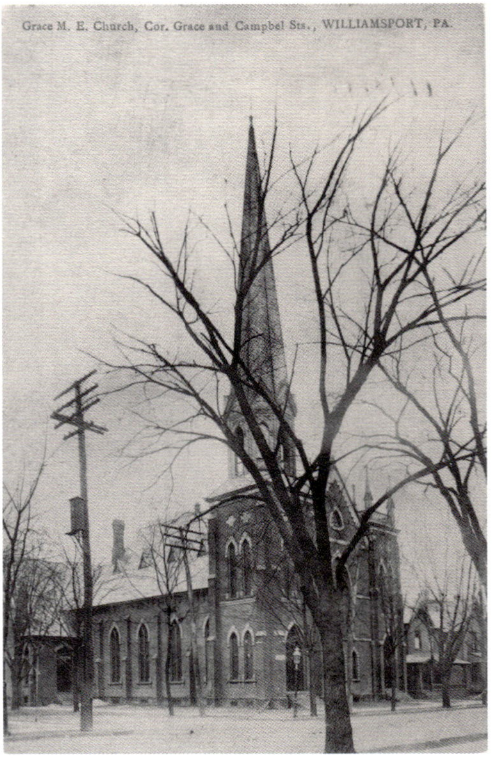

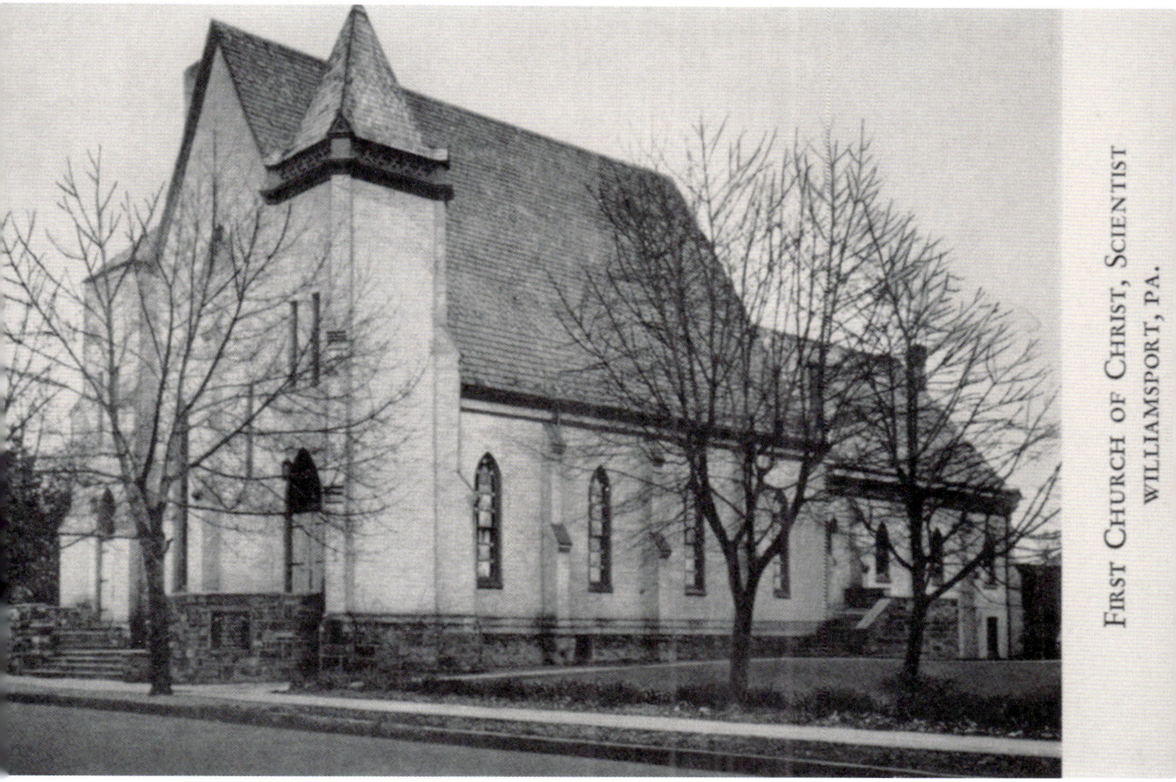

The corner of Maynard and West Third Streets was occupied by the Third Presbyterian Church in 1869. The First Church of Christ, Scientist, purchased the church and the lot in 1910. It had originally stated its intent was to build a new church on the corner of West Third Street, but it never did. Today, the church is occupied by the Gap Fellowship Church.

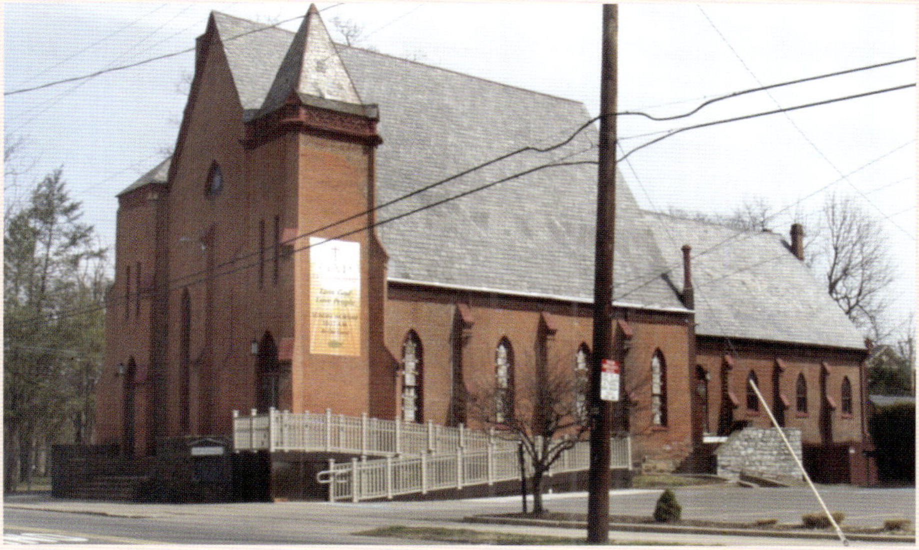

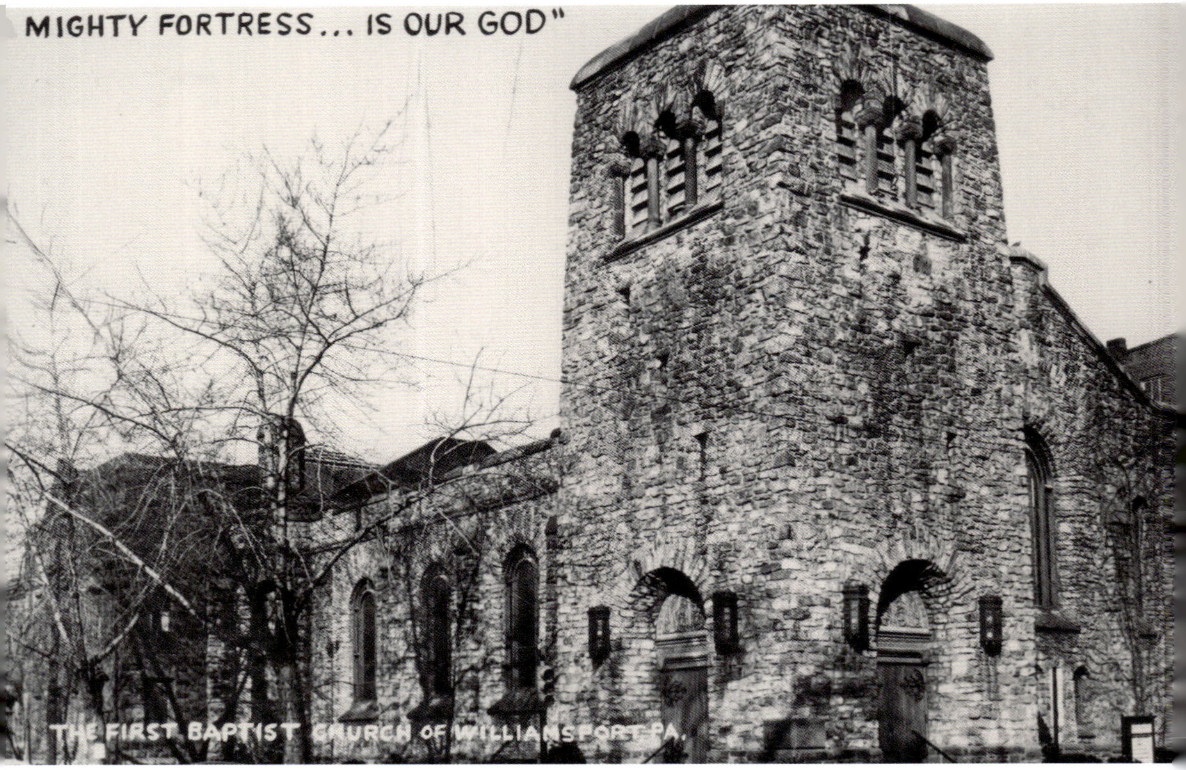

The First Baptist Church was organized in Williamsport in 1854. Its first church was at this site in 1859; however, the 1889 flood destroyed it. The church built a chapel in 1894 on two lots it purchased to the north of the original church. The current church, seen here, was attached to that chapel and dedicated in 1914. In 2015, the City Alliance Church entered a partnership with First Baptist Church to make the church and chapel its new home.

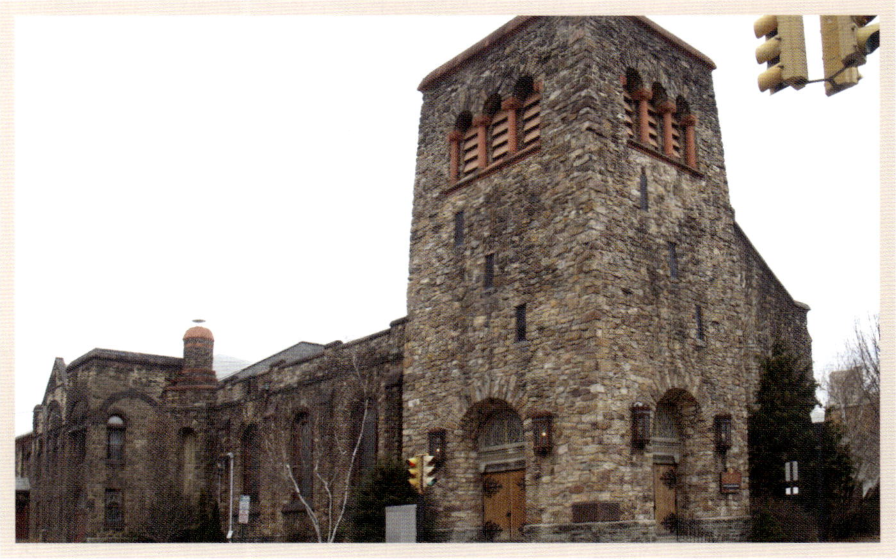

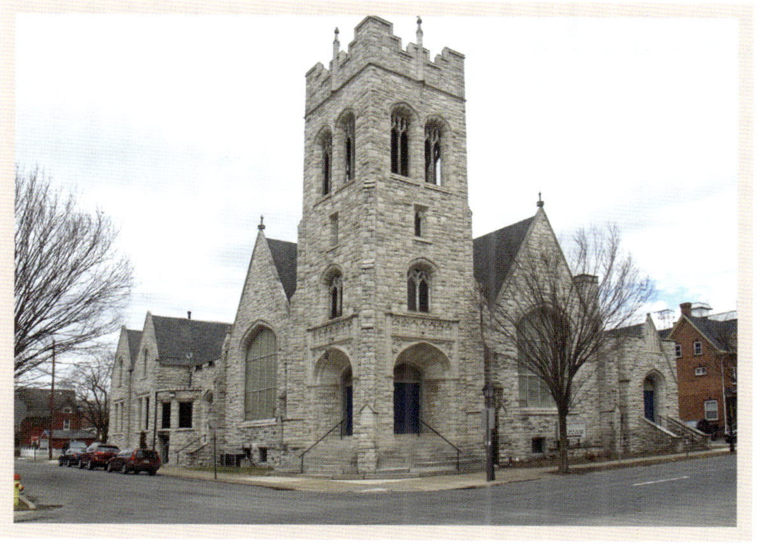

The former Presbyterian Church of the Covenant, built in the 1890s, stands at the corner of Center and West Fourth Streets. It later became St. Paul's Lutheran Church and, most recently, Christ Community Worship Center. Prior to the church building, an octagonal house occupied this site. Although no photographs are known to exist of the unique house, the shape can be seen on several old maps.

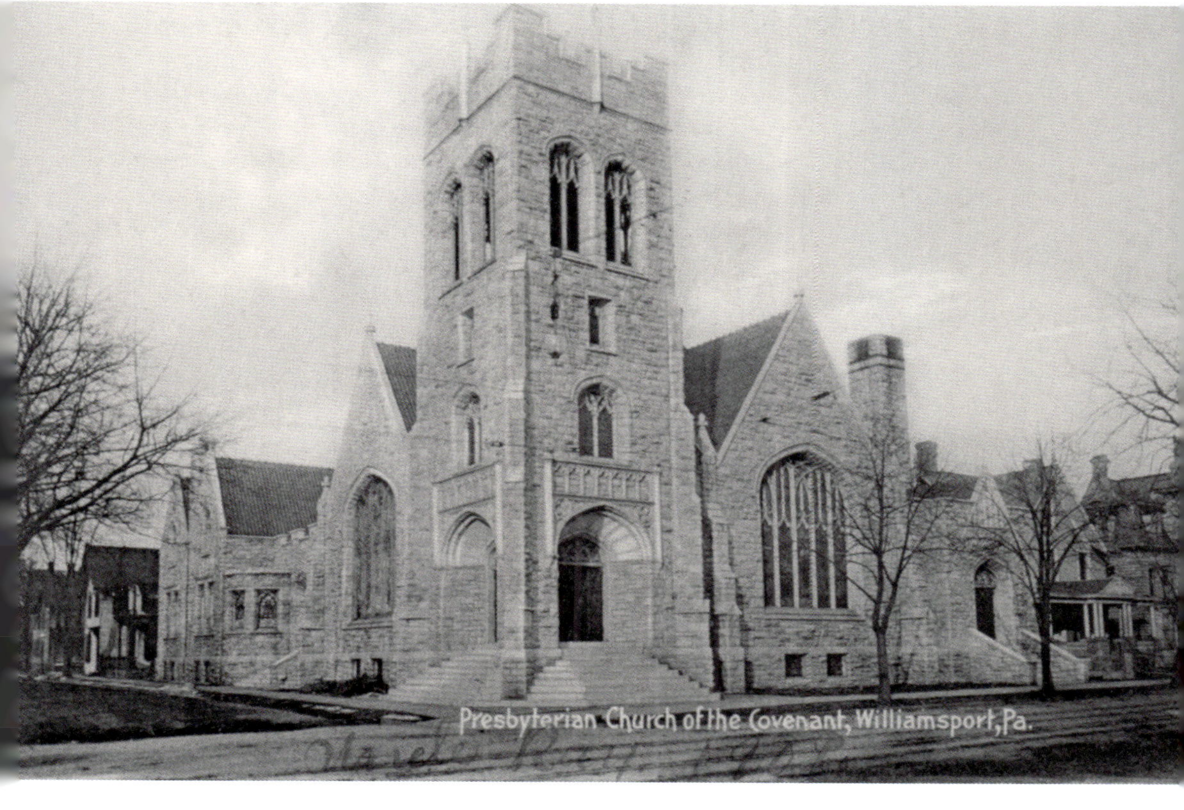

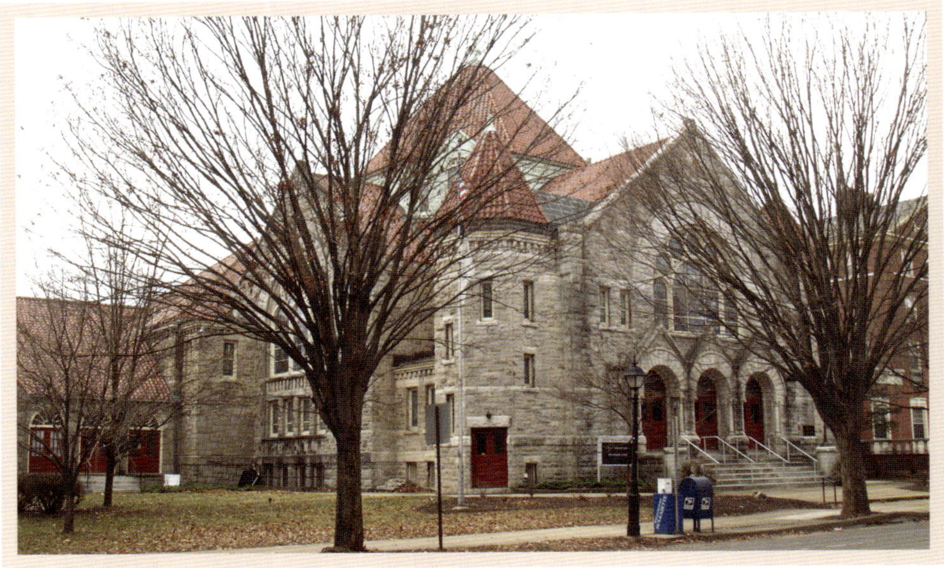

Central Presbyterian Church, as it was called then, was built in 1910. It was divided into three separate areas each with its own entrance. The church auditorium, the bible school auditorium, and the social auditorium with a kitchen and dining room represented the three areas of church life: worship, instruction, and fellowship. Today, the Covenant Central Presbyterian Church is still located at 807 West Fourth Street.

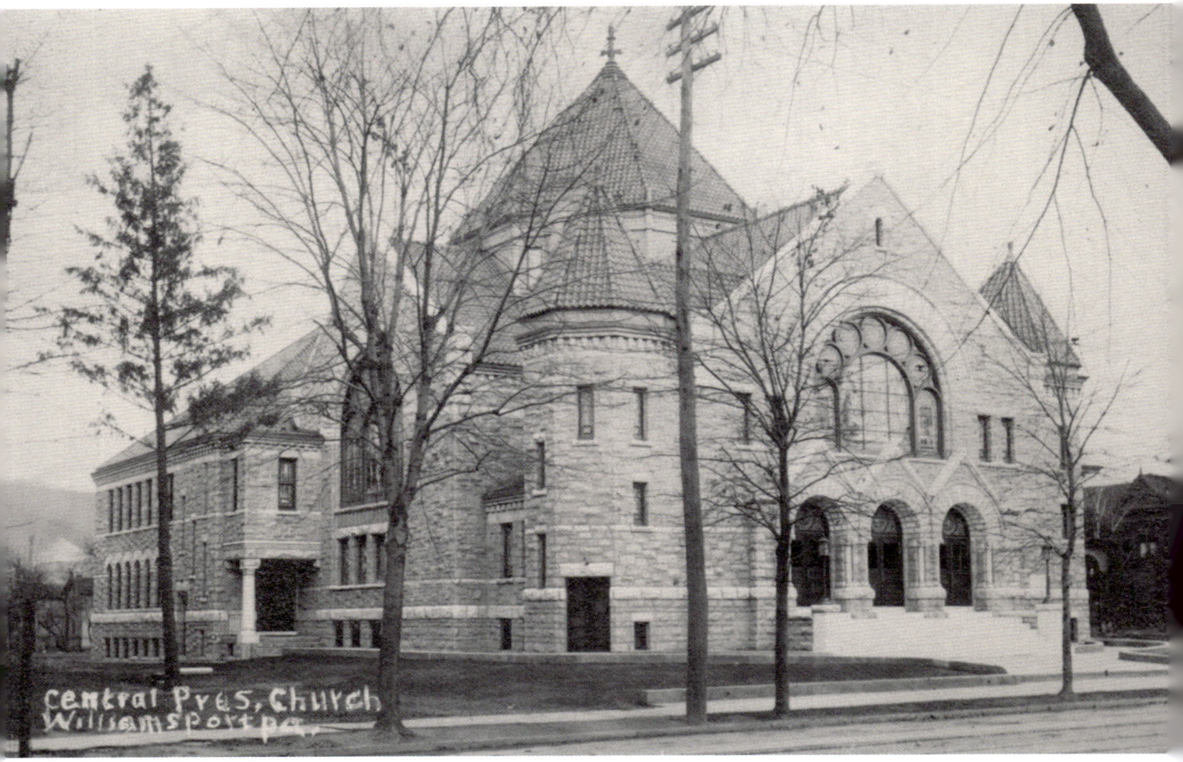

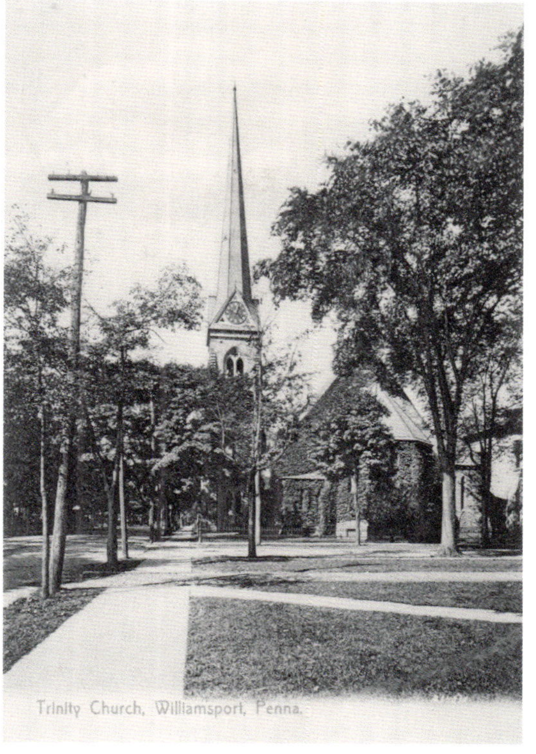

The cornerstone for the Trinity Episcopal Church on West Fourth Street was laid in 1871. The first services were in 1876, and they have continued there ever since. During the dedication, Peter Herdic presented the deed for the lot and building. He also donated the organ and tower clock. The Westminster chimes were donated to the church by Judge John W. Maynard. Today, besides the main church, there are also the parish house with a gymnasium and the chapel at this site.

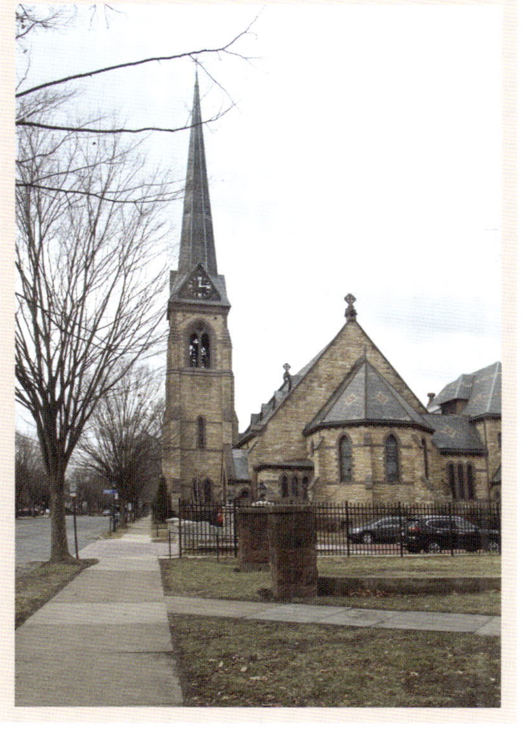

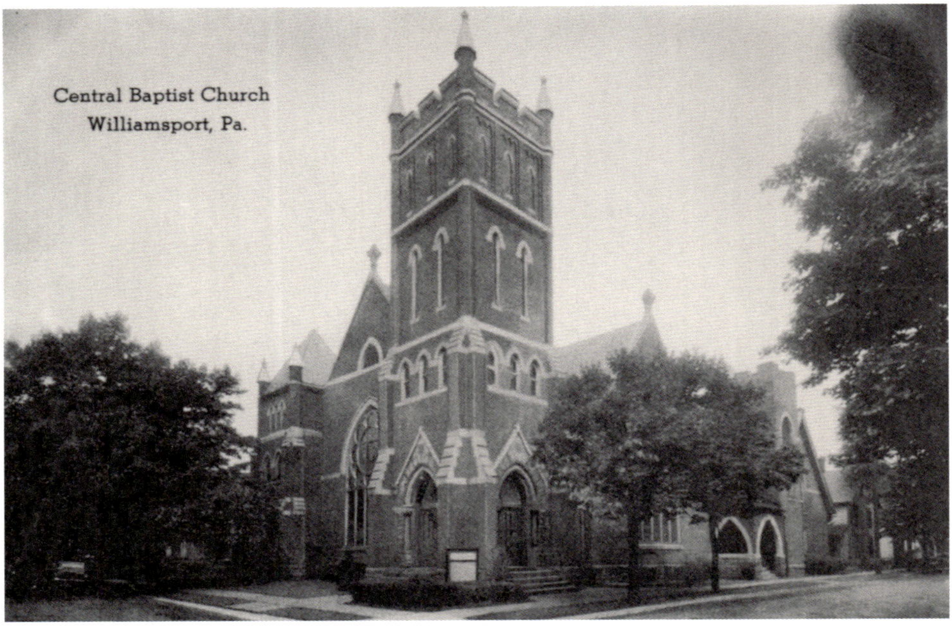

In 1887, the Newberry and West End Baptist congregations merged to become Bethel Baptist Church, then later, Erie Avenue Baptist Church. It built its first frame church at this site on the corner of Seventh Avenue. In 1891, the church decided to build a new brick church. The name of the street on the corner changed from Erie Avenue to Memorial Avenue, so by 1925, it became Central Baptist Church, which it still is today.

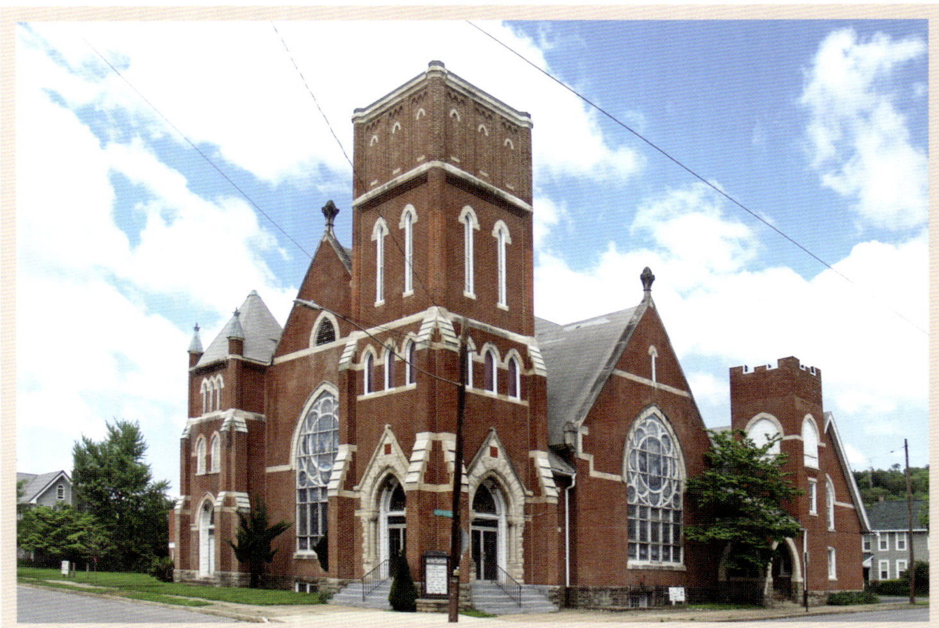

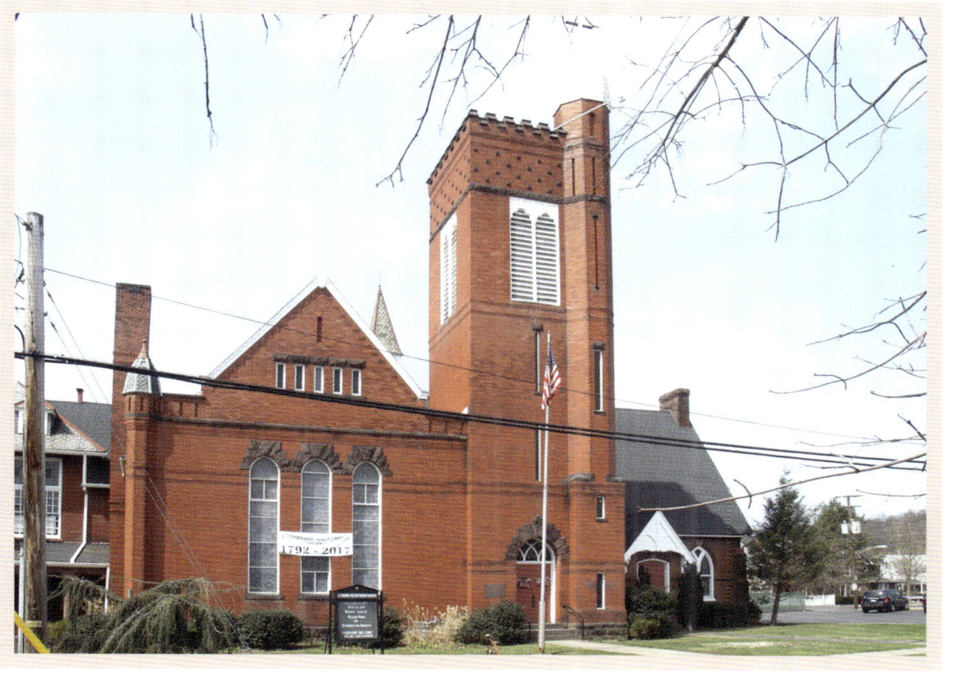

The Lycoming Presbyterian Church, still at this location on Arch Street, built its current brick church in 1891 to replace the 1850 brick church that the congregation had outgrown. Attached on the north side is the much older structure that is now the north wing of the present church. The Christian education center was joined to the south side of the building in 1925. The parsonage on the right in the vintage photograph is no longer there.

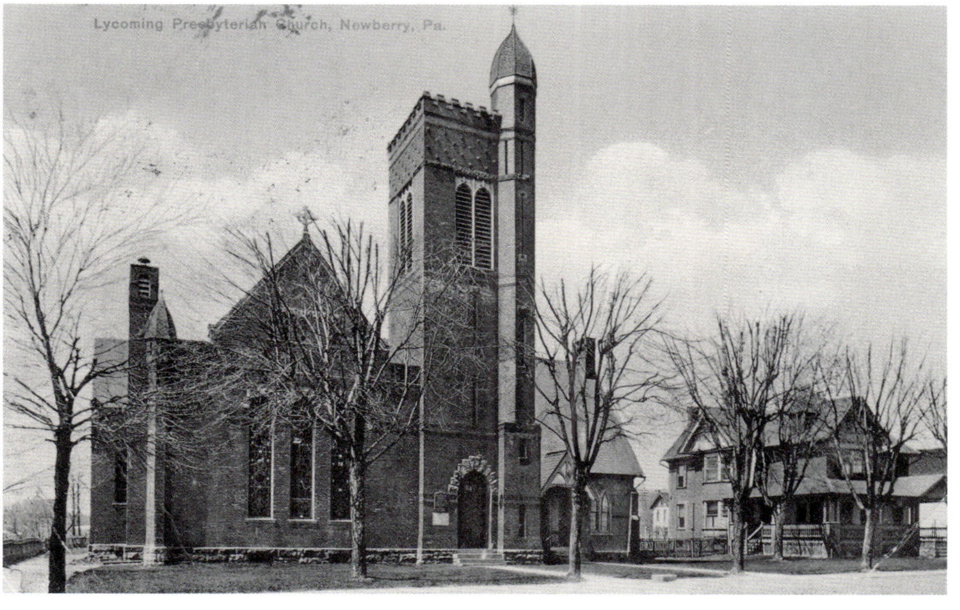

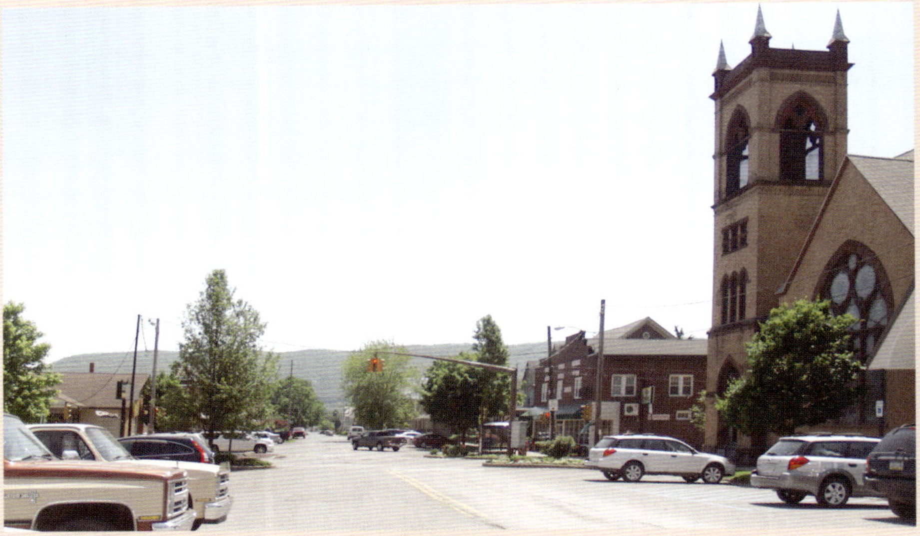

Newberry Methodist Episcopal Church, at the corner of Diamond and West Fourth Streets, was built when the older church on this site was torn down in 1898. To the north, just out of view, is the parsonage that was built in 1916. In 2004, St. John's and Newberry merged to become St. John's–Newberry United Methodist Church. This location is now the West End Christian Community Center, an outreach ministry of St. John's–Newberry UMC.

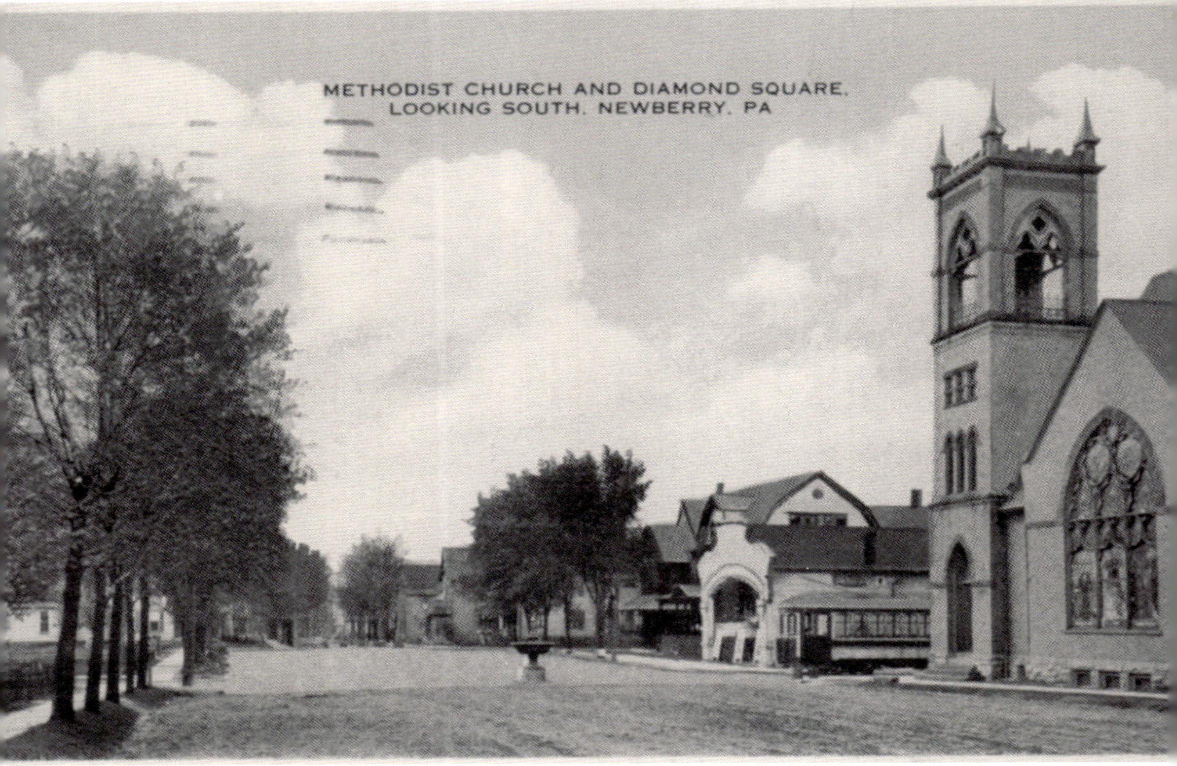

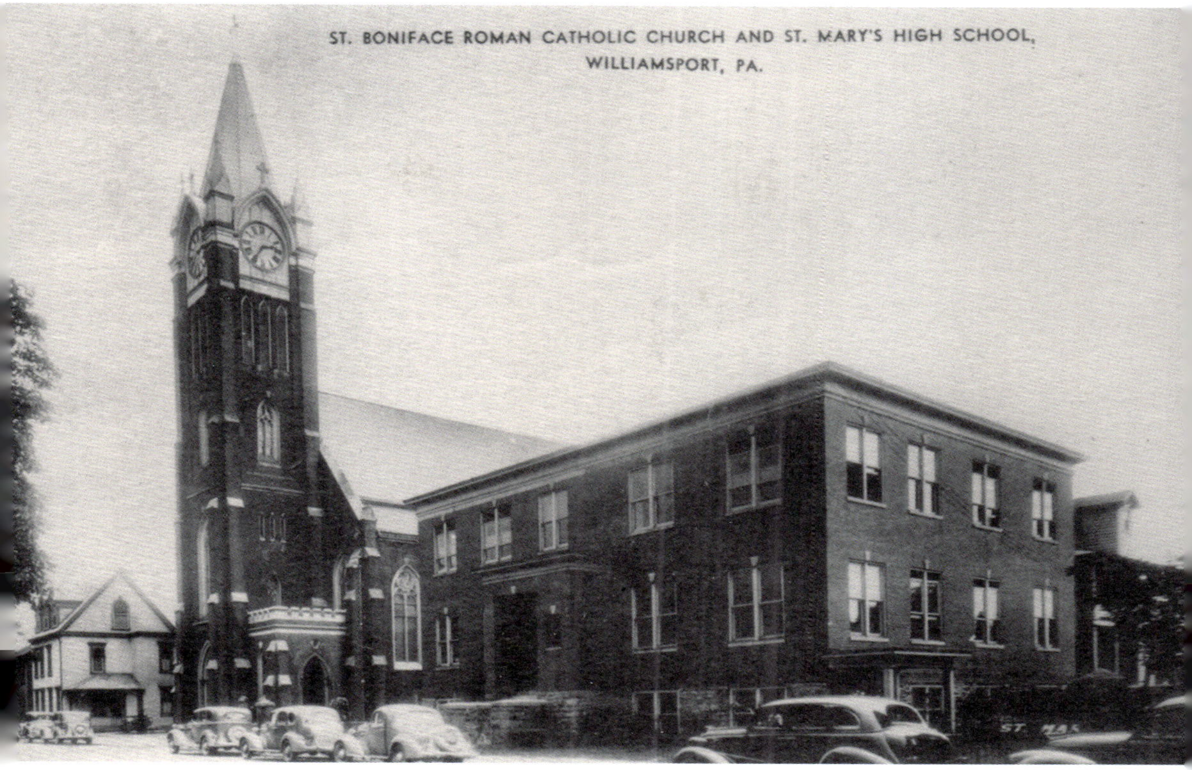

A brick church replaced the first St. Boniface Catholic Church at this site on Washington Boulevard in 1875. It had a tower that was enlarged in 1908 to rise to 145 feet. The interior of the church was decorated with a marble high altar with a portrayal of the Last Supper sculpted below. There were two side altars and several marble statues. In 1972, a fire destroyed the church. The parish rebuilt, and the current church was dedicated in 1975.

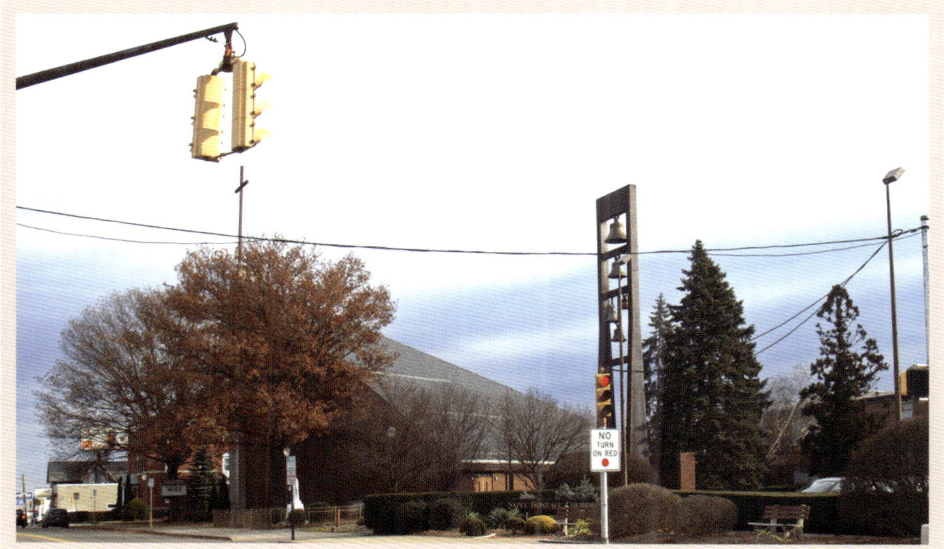

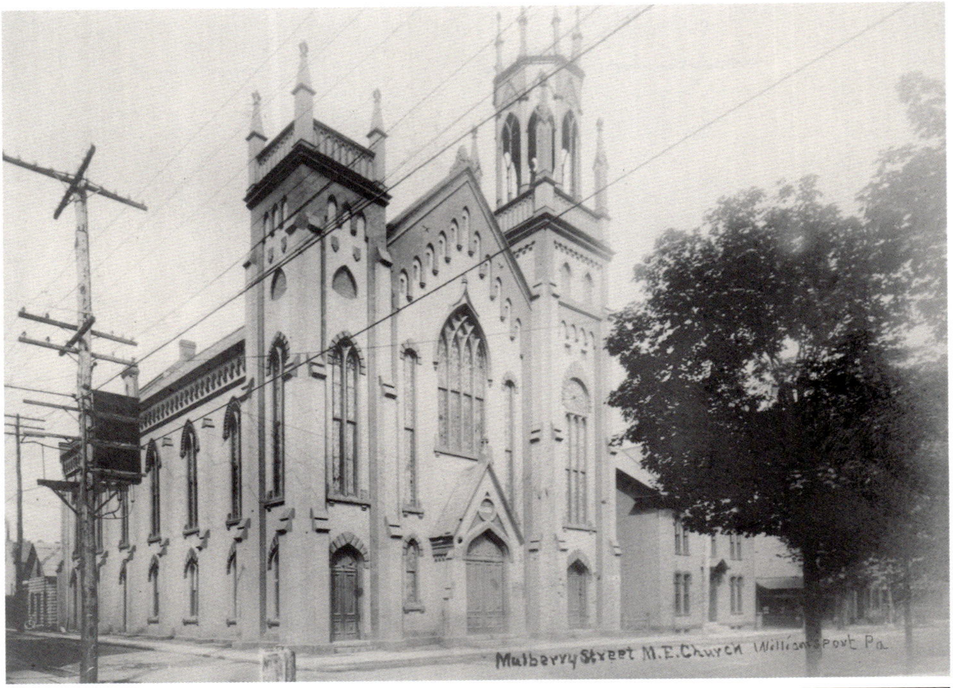

Mulberry Street Methodist Church was built in 1864 and burned in 1868. It was rebuilt in 1871 and was destroyed by fire soon after. It was again rebuilt in 1872. In 1876, a windstorm demolished the spire. The church survived, but the spire was never rebuilt. In 1963, the congregation merged with Market Street Methodist, so it sold this church. Faith Tabernacle occupied it until 1973, when it became a parking lot.

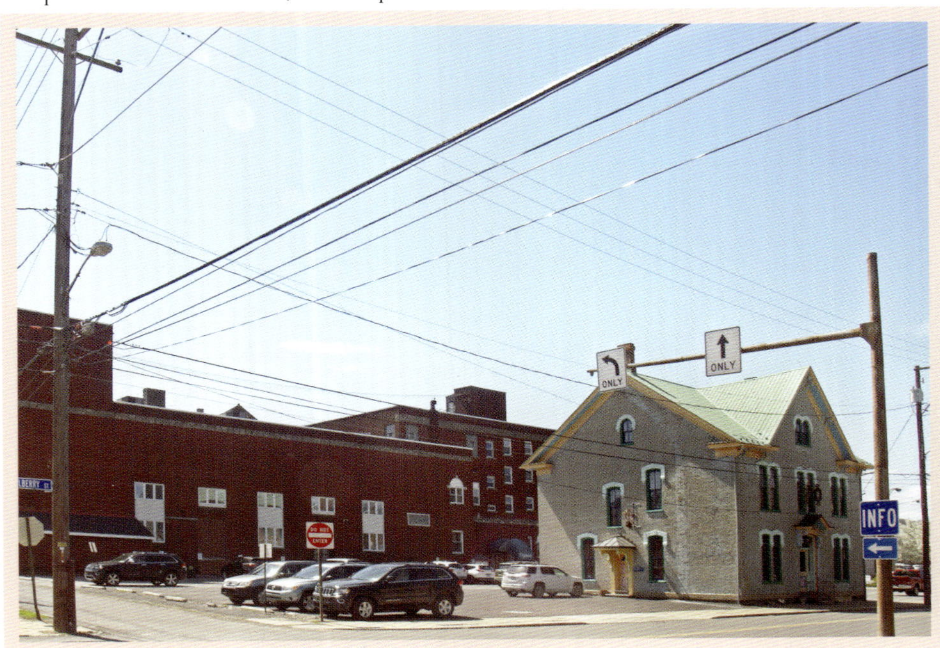

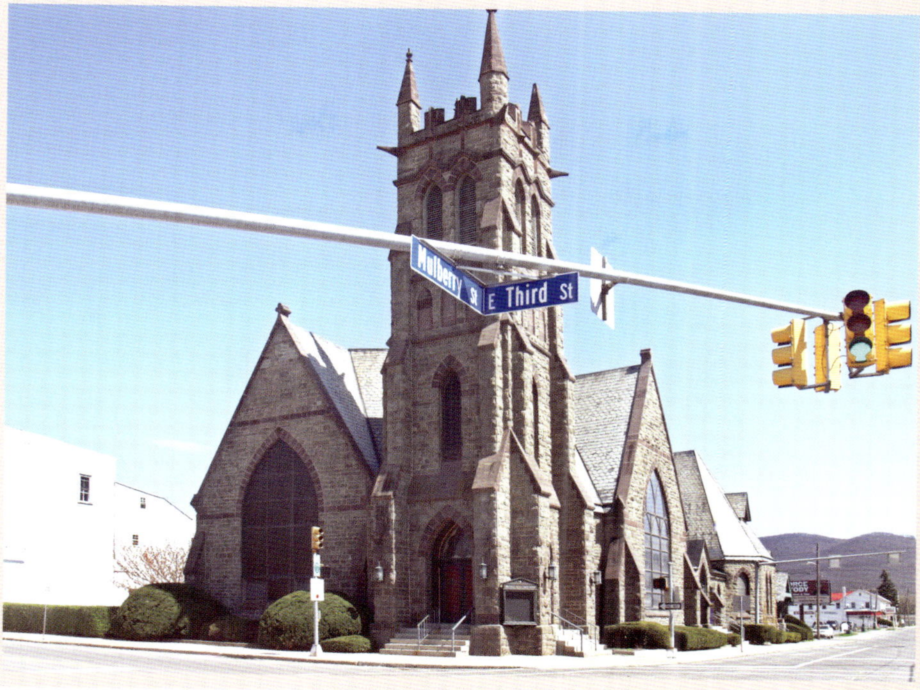

First Presbyterian built this church on the corner of Mulberry and East Third Streets in 1884. The stone structure has seen several renovations. It was repainted and equipped with electric lighting in 1903. In 1908, the tall spire was razed due to its deteriorating condition, not the least of which was grass and plants growing on it. Another renovation in 1961 included the demolition of the old parsonage. First Presbyterian had its last regular service here in February 2018.

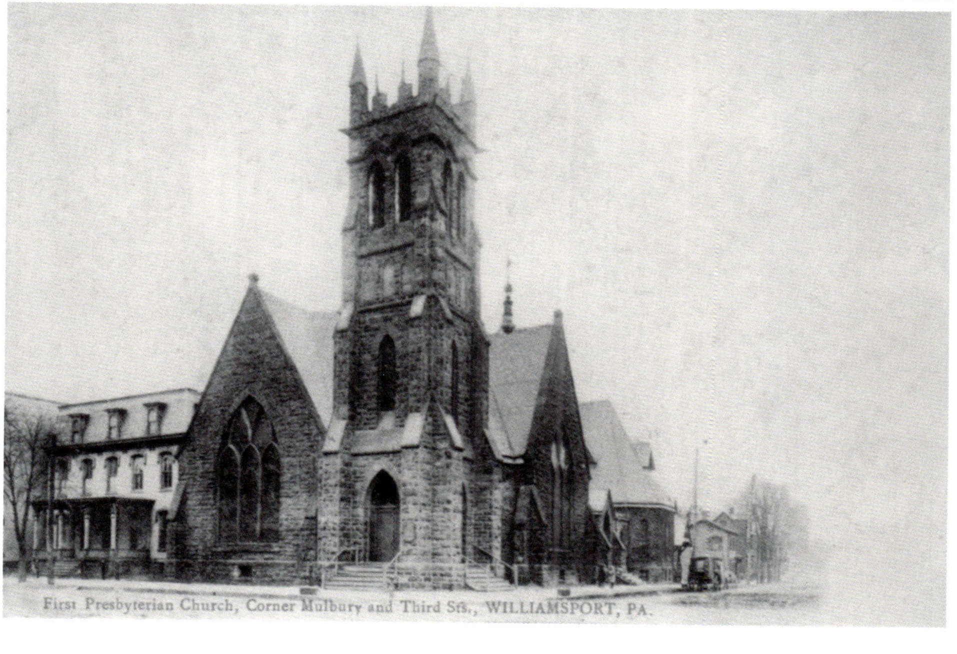

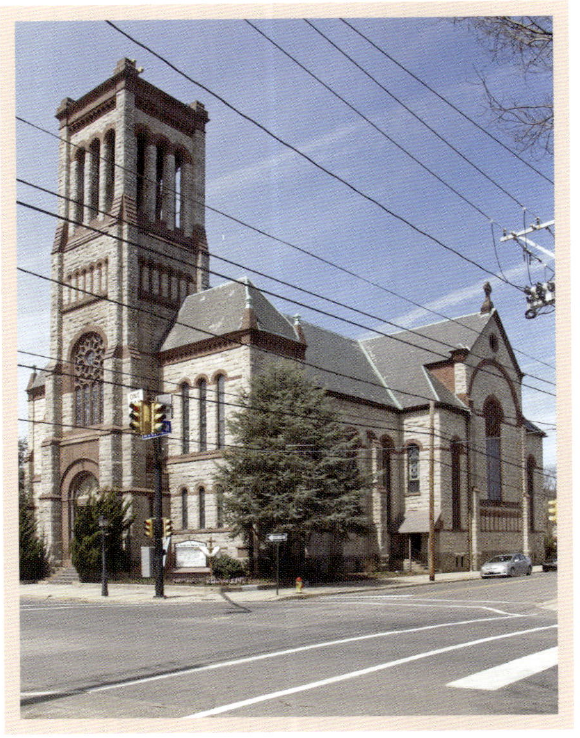

The Church of the Annunciation, now St. Joseph the Worker, was finished in 1889. Built on the corner of Walnut and West Fourth Streets, it sits just east of the original church, which later became a chapel until St. Joseph's School replaced it. Unlike many of the churches in Williamsport, Annunciation never had a high steeple, though it was originally planned. During construction, the scaffolding collapsed, killing four men. Father Eugene A. Garvey, the pastor, ordered the tower capped at that height.

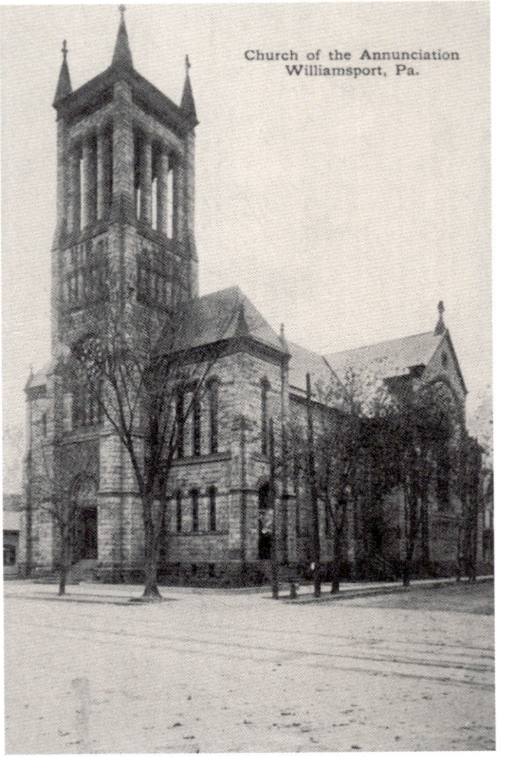

CHAPTER 6

Homes

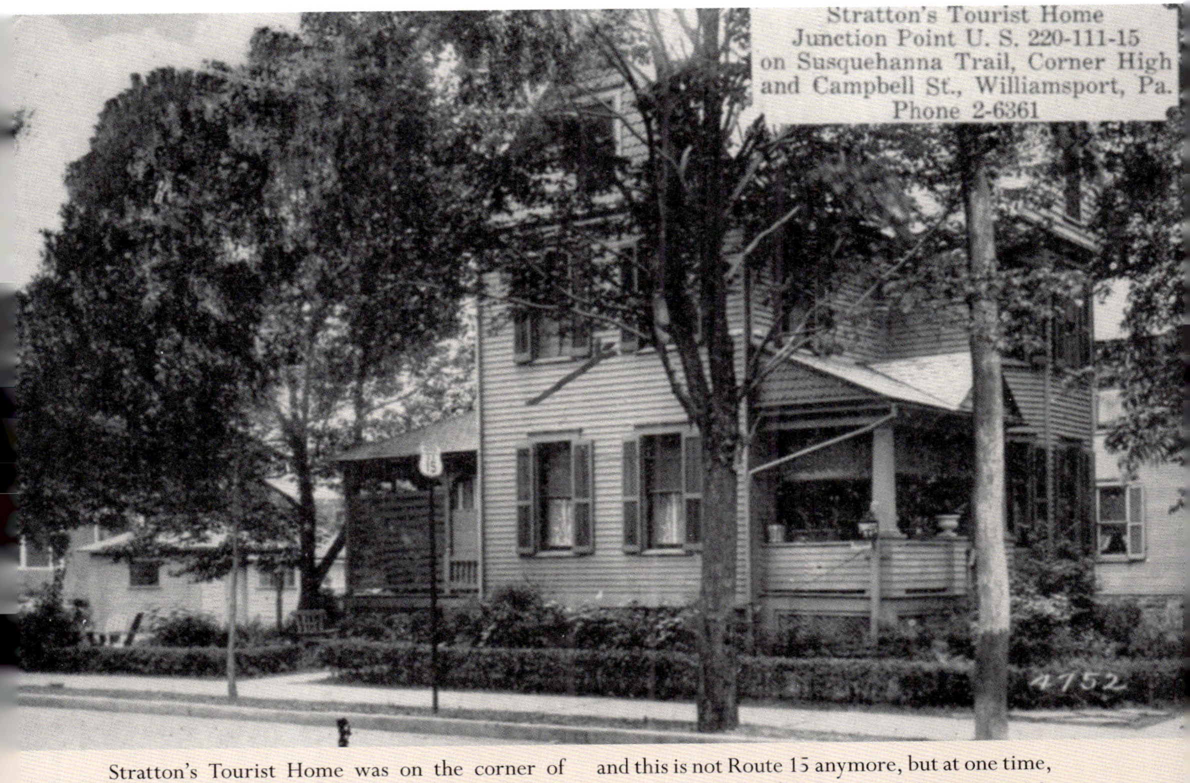

Stratton's Tourist Home was on the corner of Campbell and High Streets. Along busy Route 15, the Strattons also ran a radio and TV service business from here. The house is no longer there, and this is not Route 15 anymore, but at one time, before it became a parking area for the hospital, this area was a neighborhood filled with homes.

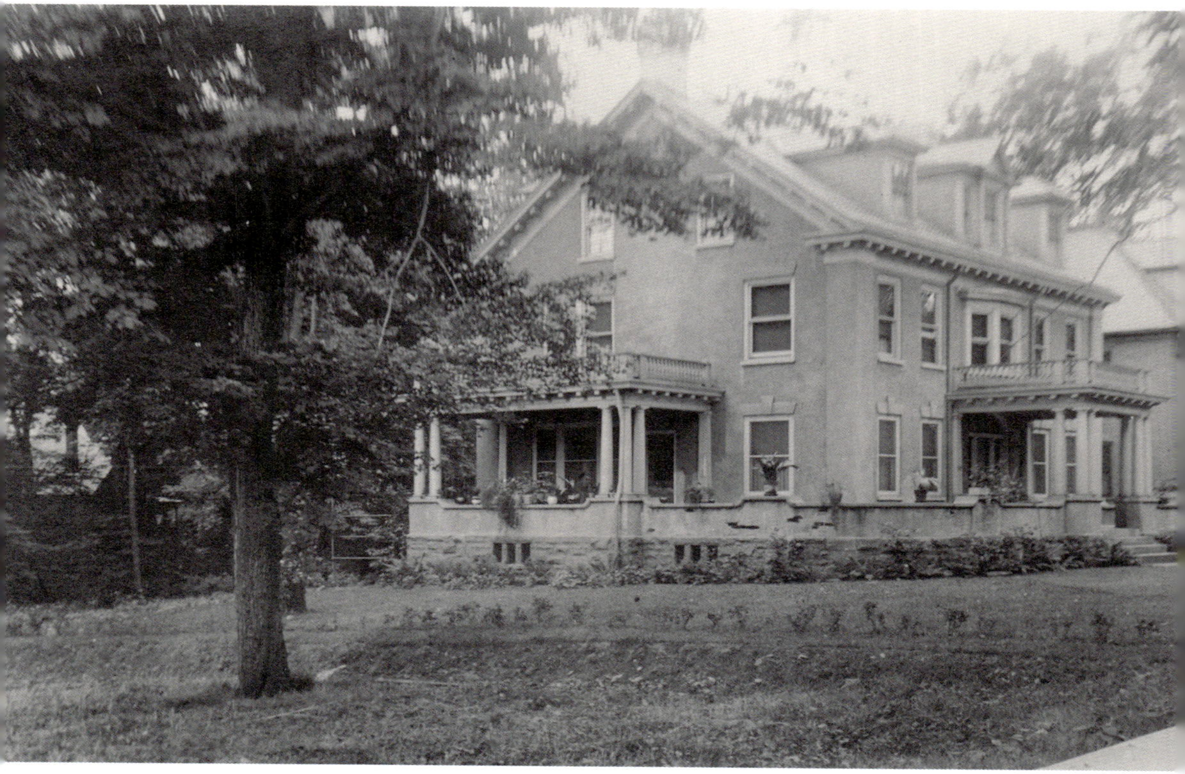

George D. Gingrich, president of National Foundry Manufacturing, broke ground for his new home on Rural Avenue in November 1911. The postcard above was sent from the family in December 1922 to wish the recipient a Merry Christmas and a Happy New Year and to invite them for a visit. Four months later, Gingrich contracted tuberculosis. He died on October 13, 1923, at the age of 59.

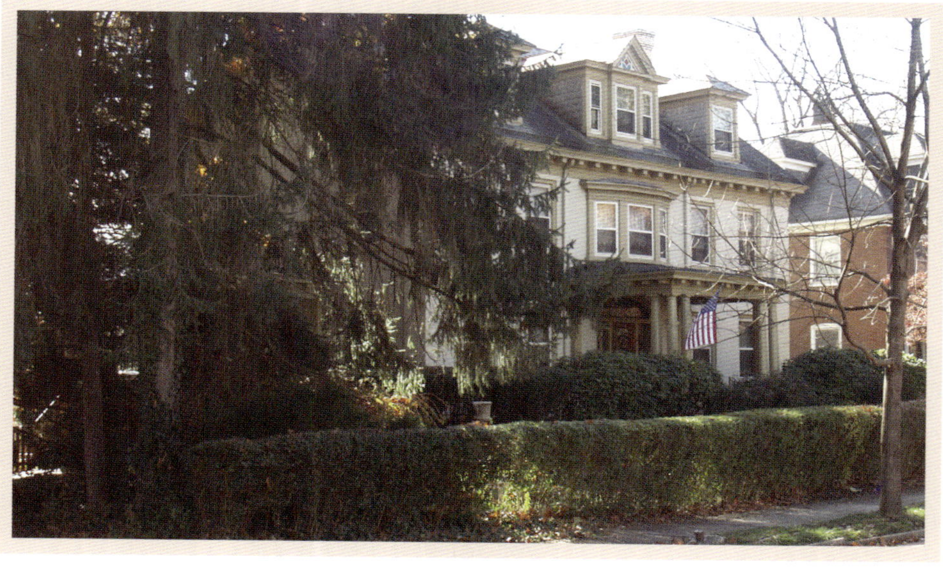

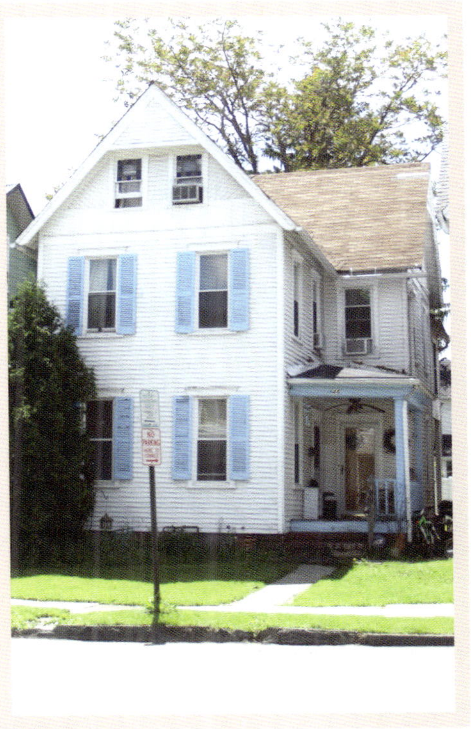

Gustav Kliemann was a well-known and respected music authority in Williamsport. He lived here on Washington Boulevard from 1902 until his death in 1937, after which time his daughter resided here. His Williamsport School of Music, at this same location, offered instrumental and voice lessons. Kliemann was the Gesang Verein Harmonia chorus director for many years, as well as director of the mandolin orchestra at the high school. In 1952, the Williamsport Symphony Society dedicated a concert in his memory.

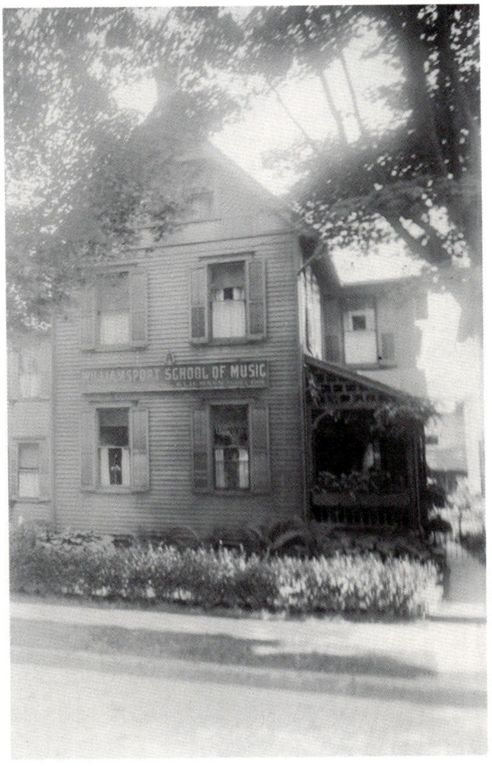

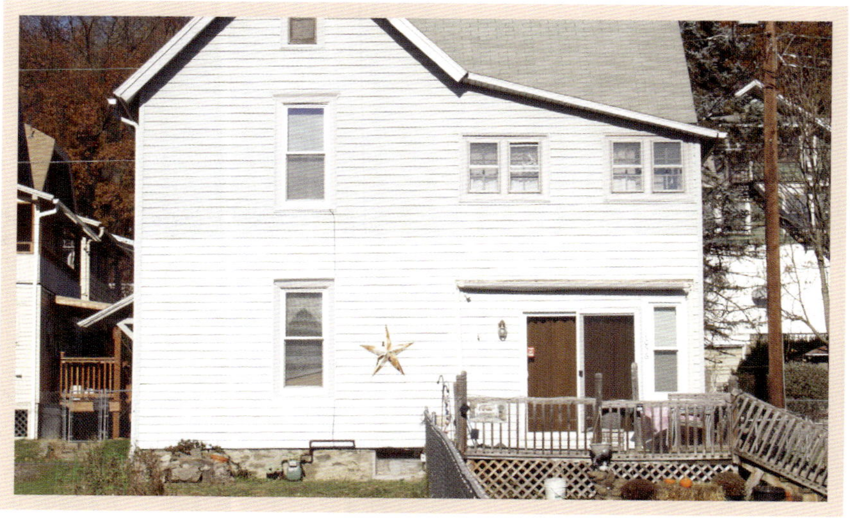

The photograph of this home on High Street from the 1920s doesn't show the unusually long front yard. The house has remained almost the same except for the enlarged second floor above the now closed-in porch. Mary Shick can be seen looking out at her son Franklin in the vintage photograph. Mary lived here with her husband, Adam, until her death in 1951. Franklin grew up to serve in World War II. After being discharged, he became a teacher.

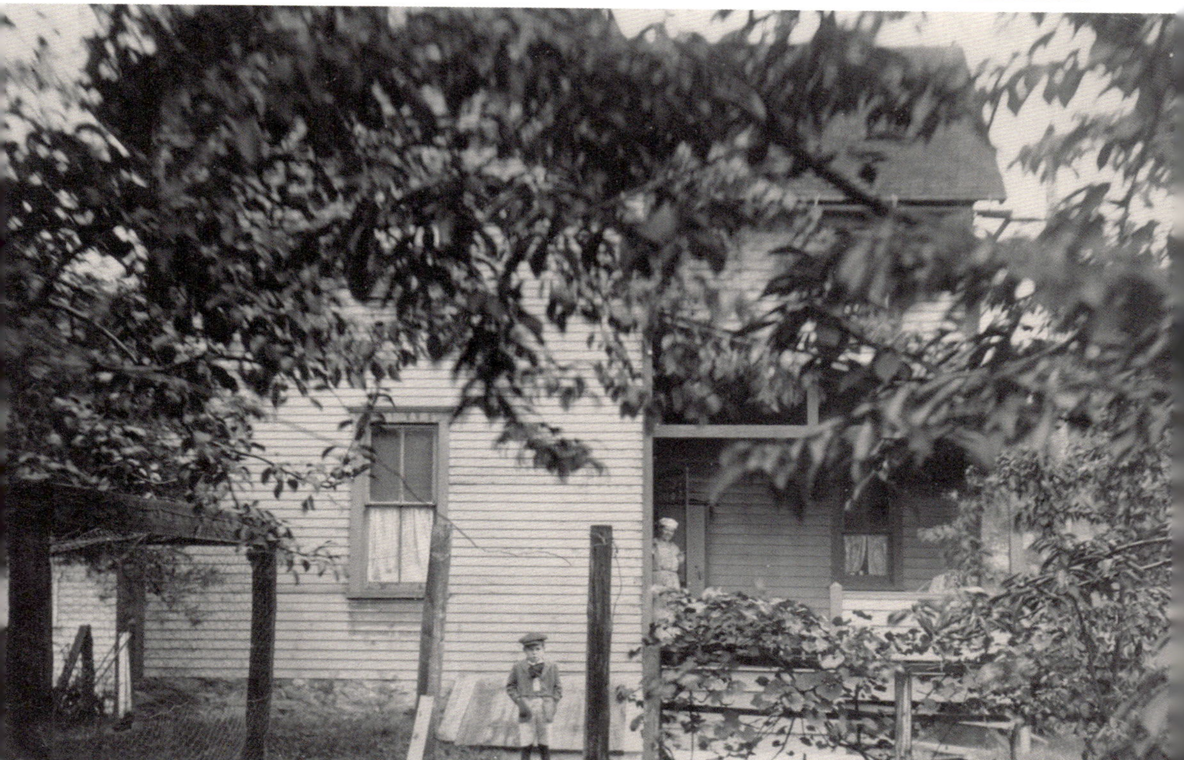

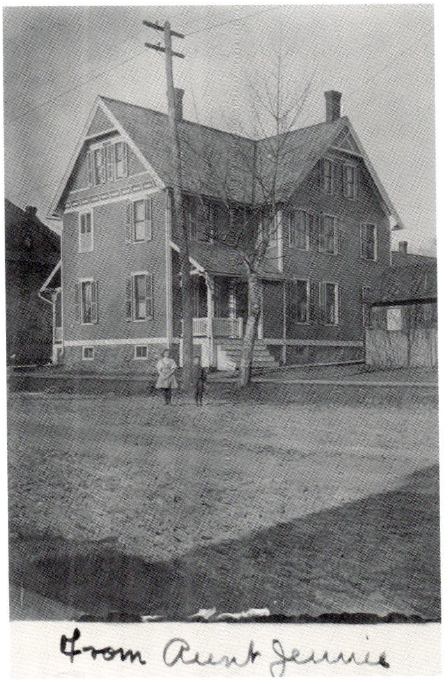

The exterior of the house on Cherry Street has remained much the same as it was in the vintage photograph at right. This postcard was sent in 1908 from "Aunt Jennie" Dunkleberger during the short period that she and her husband, John, lived here. The children in the photograph are probably their daughter and son. The back reads, "This is where Aunt Jenny lives. Come to see me. J.E.D." Then, in smaller writing, it says, "Tell your mother I'm out of lard."

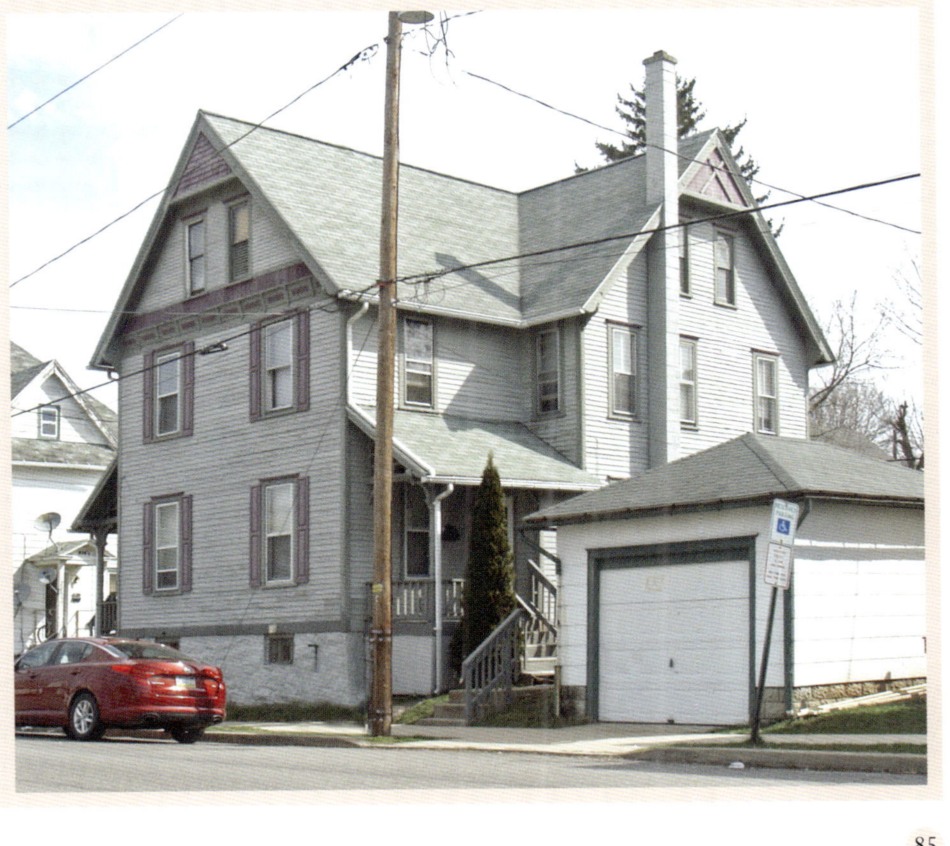

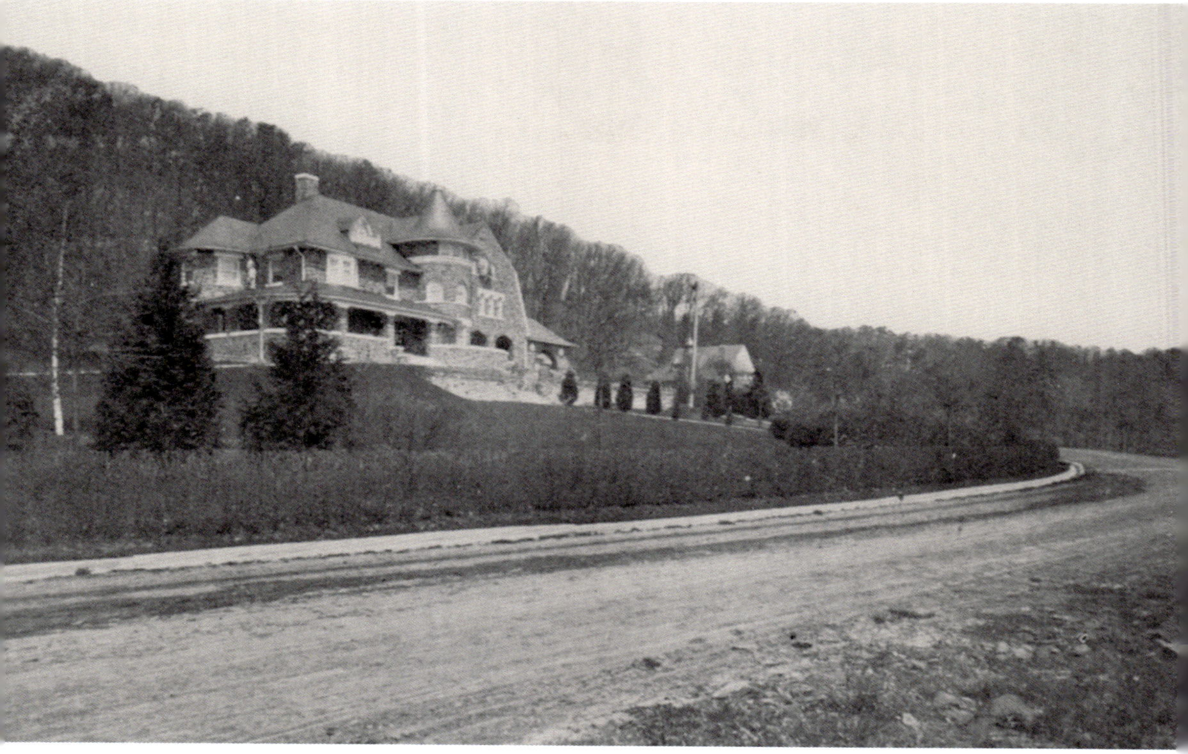

The Greystone Mansion on Vallamont Drive has over 20 rooms and more than 4,300 square feet of living space. It was built in 1902 by Allen P. Perley, the president of West Branch National Bank. He built it on the same plan as the 1890 house that was originally here but was destroyed by fire in 1893. The Perley family lived here for many years. Today, it is still a single-family dwelling, with much of its original appearance.

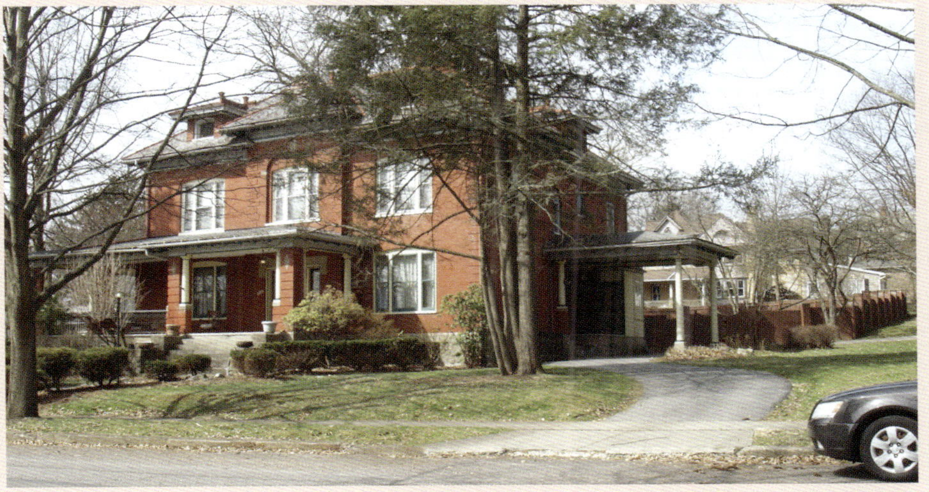

This house on Woodmont Avenue was a single-family dwelling before becoming the Felicitas Order of the Eastern Star in 1951. Established to care for the infirm members of the Eastern Star, it remained mostly unchanged except for a few state-mandated adjustments. It was able to accommodate 36 guests. From 1967 to 1976, it was the Florence Crittenton Home, which offered services and housing to unmarried mothers. Since then, it has been restored back to a large single-family home.

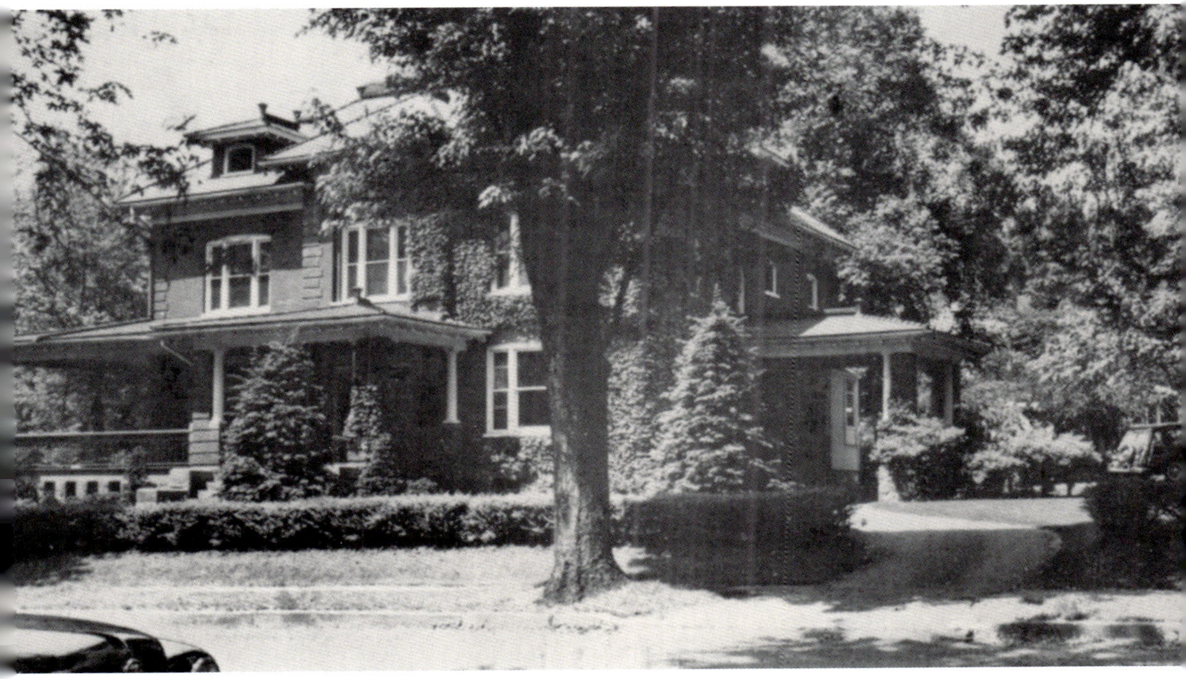

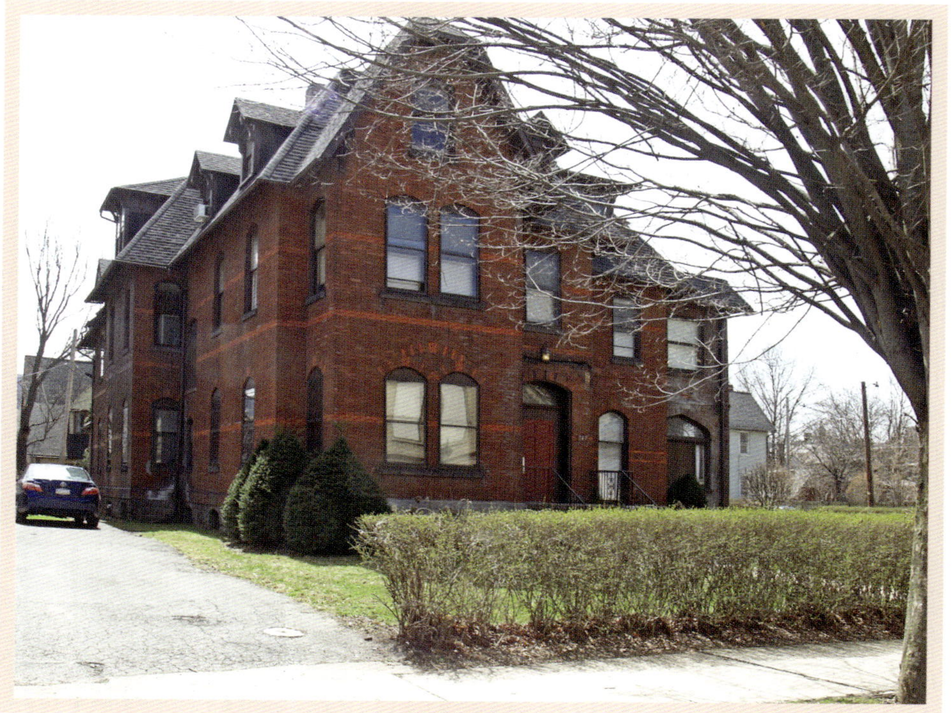

Before it was Pott's Shorthand College, this large home on West Fourth Street belonged to C. LaRue Munson, a lawyer with the firm Candor and Munson. He was also a successful businessman in many Williamsport industries. Around 1918, he relocated to the Vallamont section of Williamsport, and William Beeber, also a lawyer, became the next occupant. He lived here until it became Pott's Shorthand College around 1931. Through the years, it had many uses, most recently as apartments.

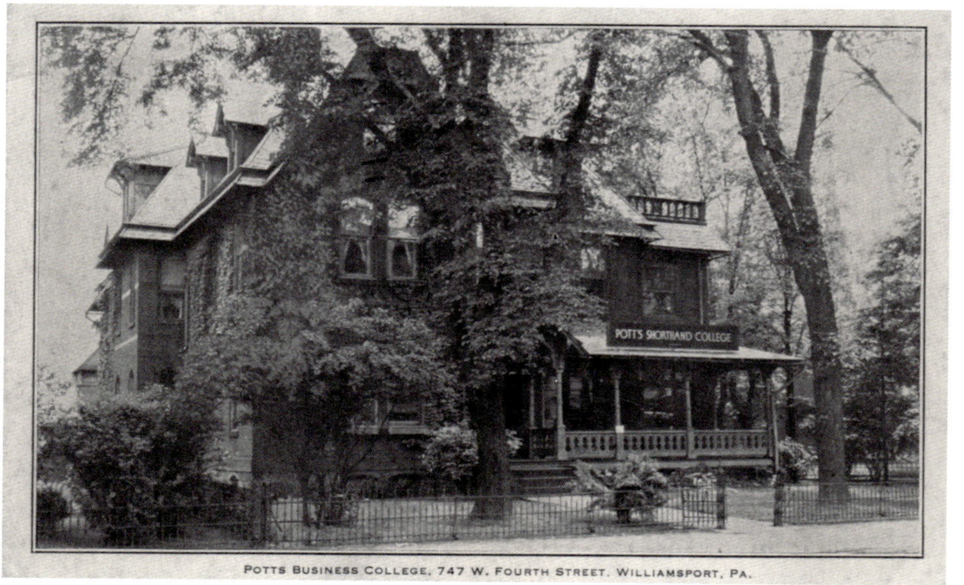

POTTS BUSINESS COLLEGE, 747 W. FOURTH STREET, WILLIAMSPORT, PA.

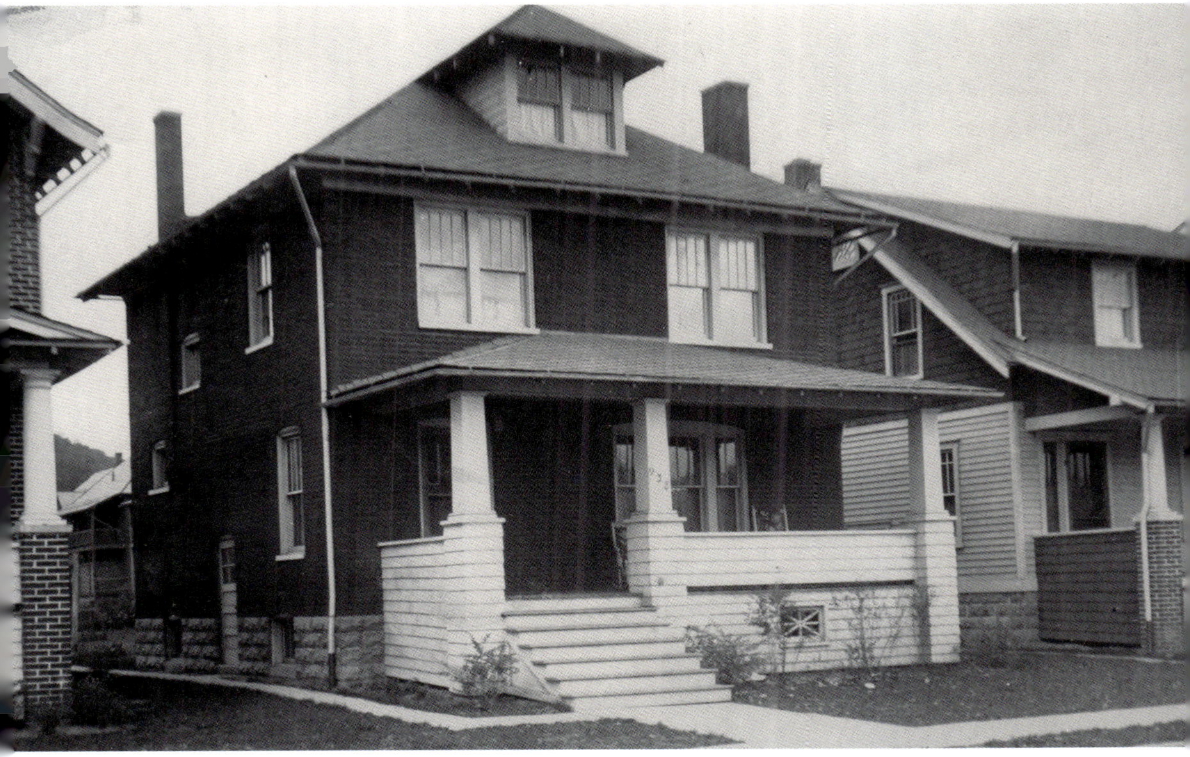

This house on Park Avenue was built around 1923. Some of the first occupants include George Swan, who managed the Edler Coal Company. A year later, Seth McCormick, owner of the Trail Garage on Hepburn Street, lived here. Dr. Charles Seaton and his wife followed and lived here for several years. Initially, this site had enough traffic and accidents to warrant a "stop-and-go" signal at the nearby intersection. Today, a two-way stop sign keeps traffic flowing safely.

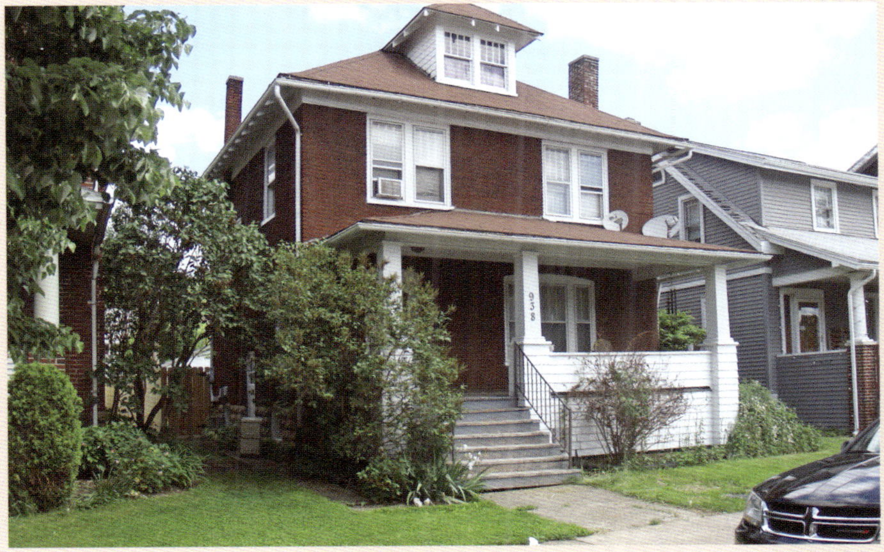

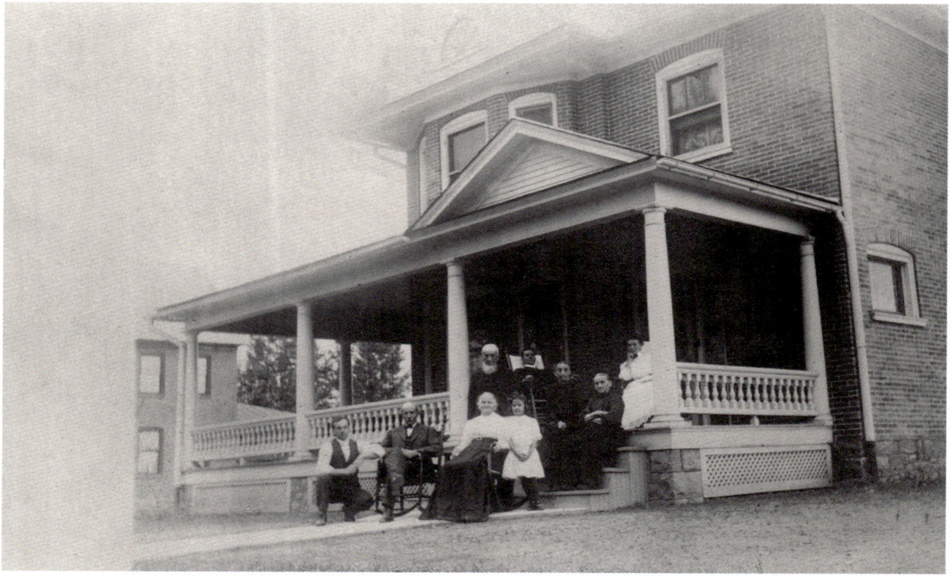

This home on Parkwood Street is presently as beautiful as the day it was built in 1909 by Dr. Jacob P. Snyder. He lived here with his wife, Sophie, and family until his death in 1923. The postcard above was sent by his wife in August 1909 with the anticipation that the recipient, Mrs. H.G. Hoover, would recognize some of the people. Although they have not yet been identified, they are probably members of the Snyder family.

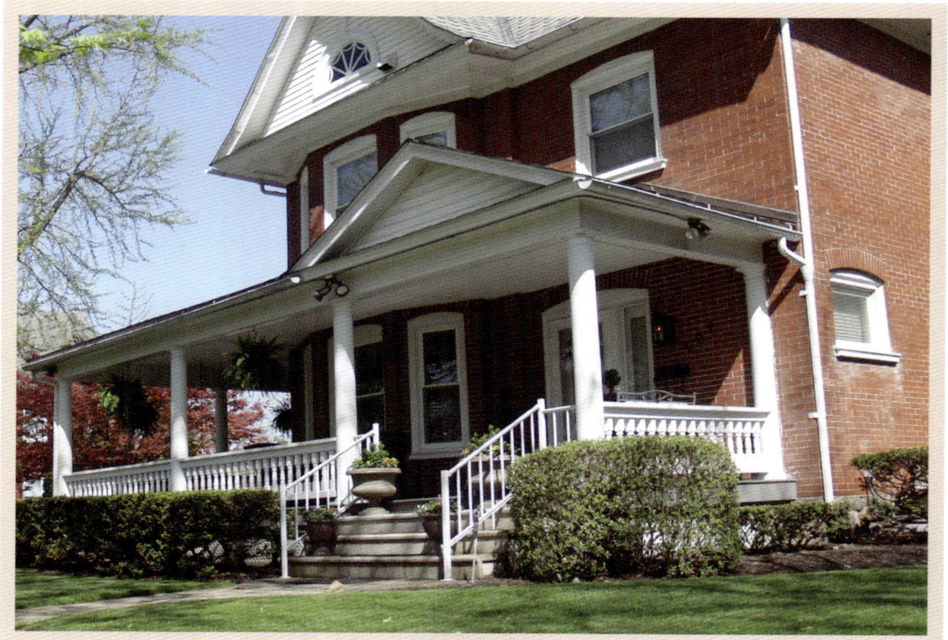

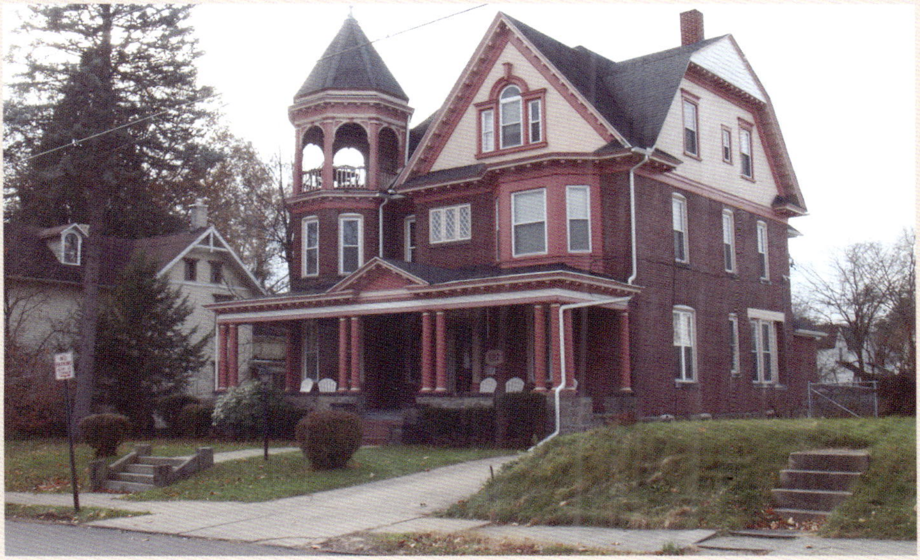

Lucy S. DeWitt moved to Williamsport and built her home on Hepburn Street in 1906 after her husband, Ira, died. She lived here until her death in 1918. Edmund Sheriff of Reese-Sheriff Lumber Company bought the house and resided here until the 1930s. It was converted to a multi-family building around 1945, and is still apartments today; the exterior has remained largely unchanged.

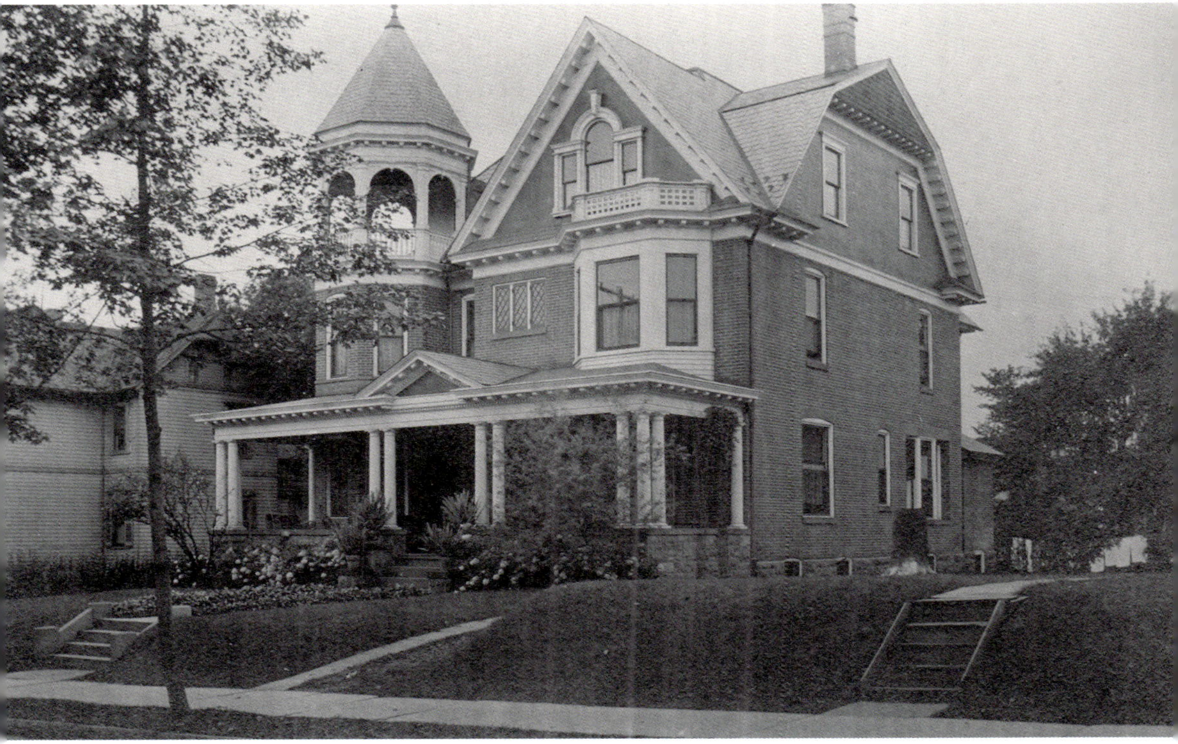

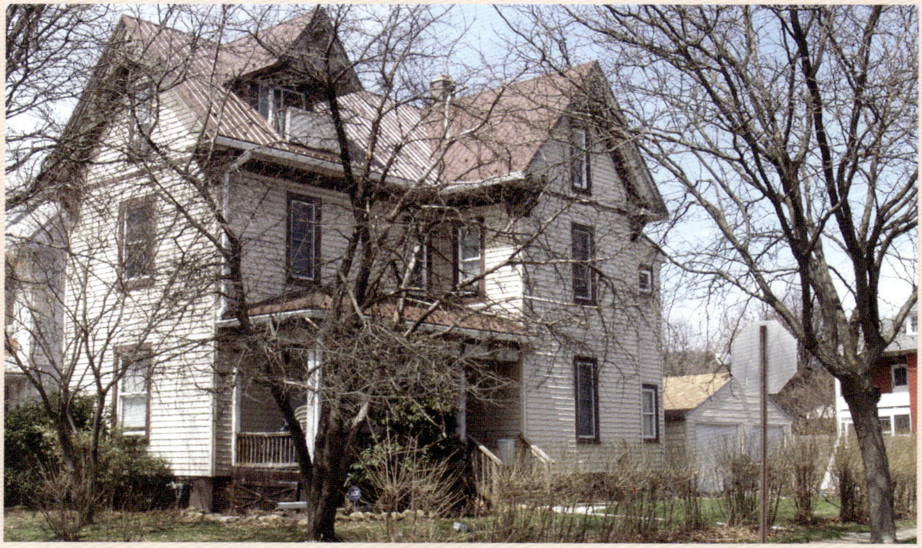

Samuel and Julia Hoffman lived here on the corner of Locust and West Edwin Streets beginning in 1893. Samuel was a wholesale lumber dealer at that time. By the early 1900s, he was running a grocery store on the corner of Locust and West Third Streets, where Bart's Pizzeria is today. The Hoffman name was on this house for almost a century. Samuel and Julia lived here for the remainder of their married life, then their son made it his family's home.

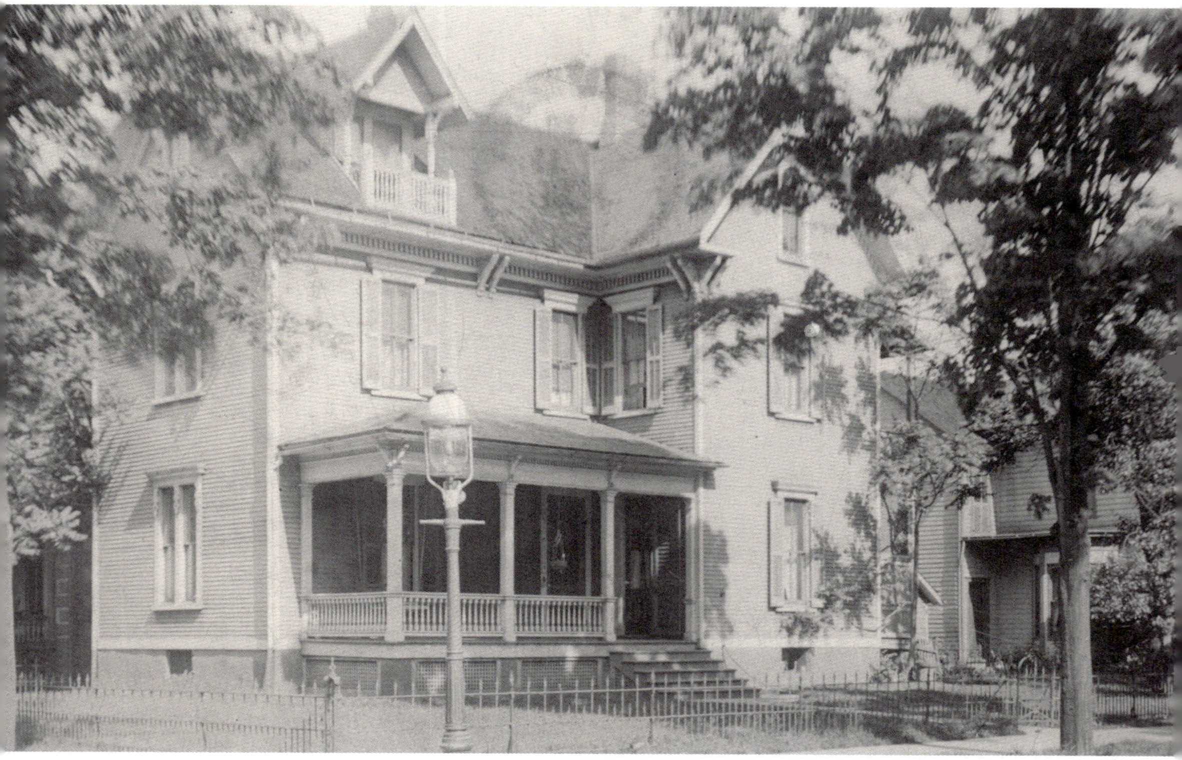

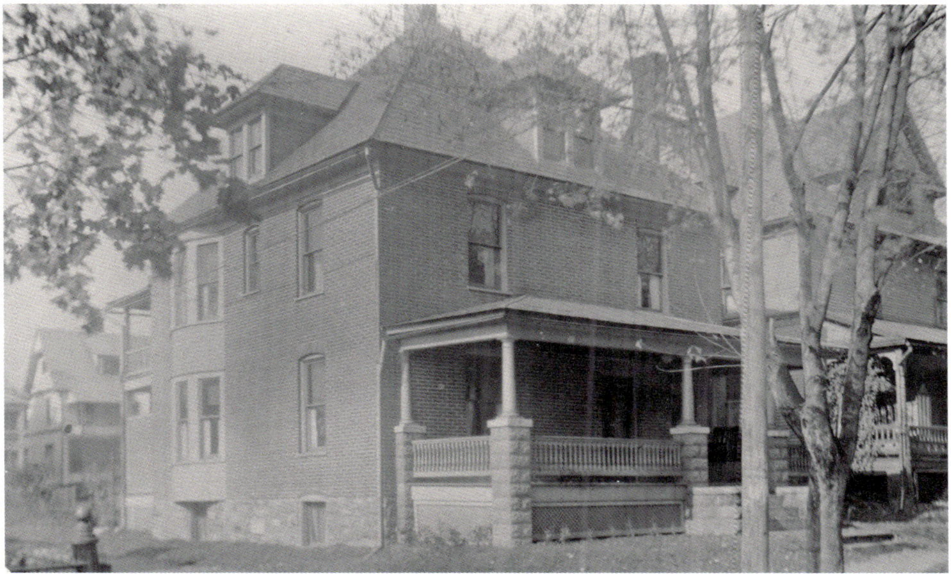

The 1916 photograph above shows the Frank Stutzman family's new house on Fourth Avenue. They lived here until the mid-1930s. In 1900, Frank constructed and patented a gasoline engine automobile at his plant on Campbell Street. It was a success, and the Stutzman Automobile Company was formed. He sold his machine plant in 1902 to A.D. Hermance and Galvin Marsch, but opened another at the foot of Locust Street, where he invented the Stutzman Round Safety Cylinder Head.

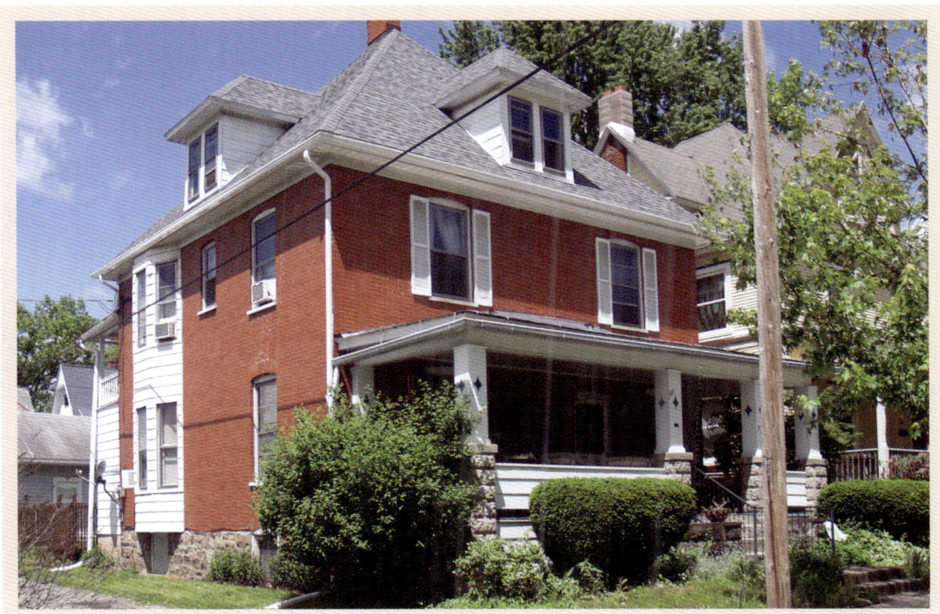

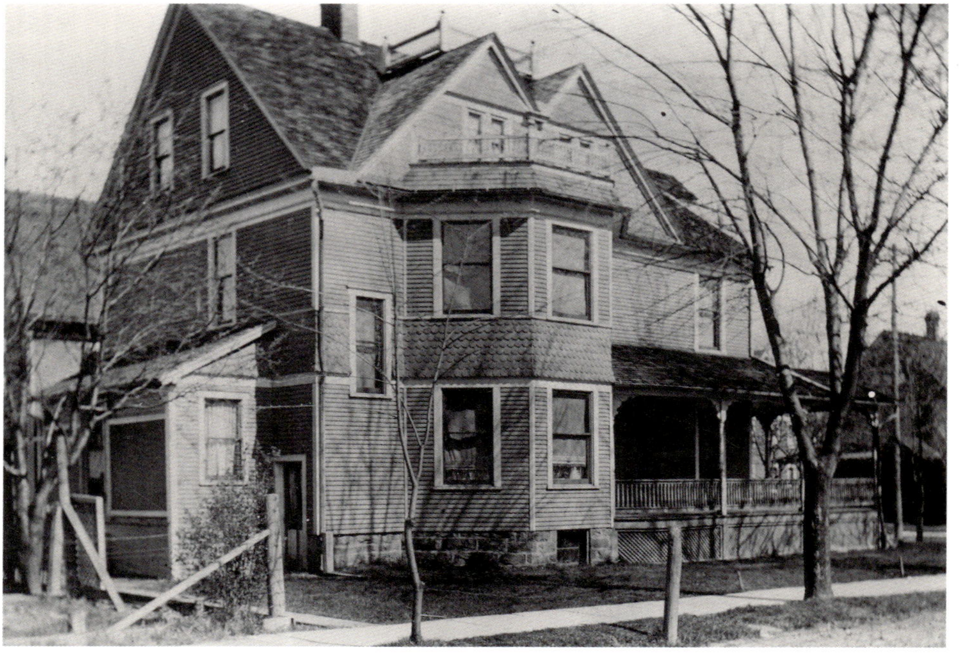

The 1909 photograph above of West Fourth Street in Newberry was sent as a postcard by Lloyd Good, a neighbor, to Roy Neuhard in Masten, Pennsylvania. Neuhard had lived here with his parents before going to the lumber mill company town of Masten, which no longer exists. He was 15 years old then. By 1911, the family was spending winters out West, where they eventually relocated.

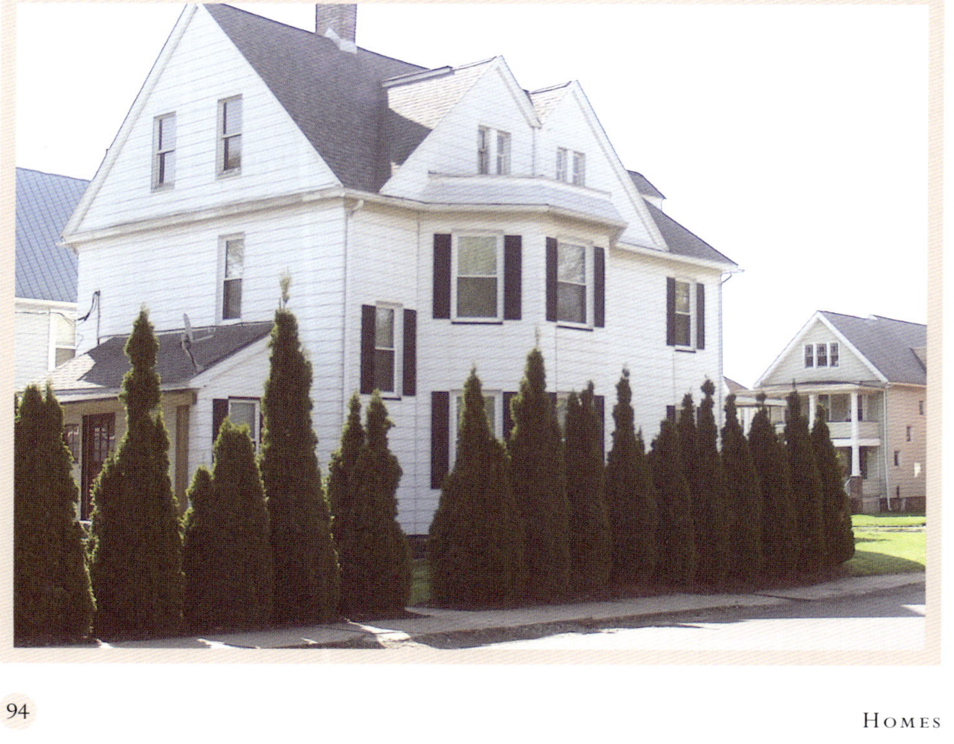

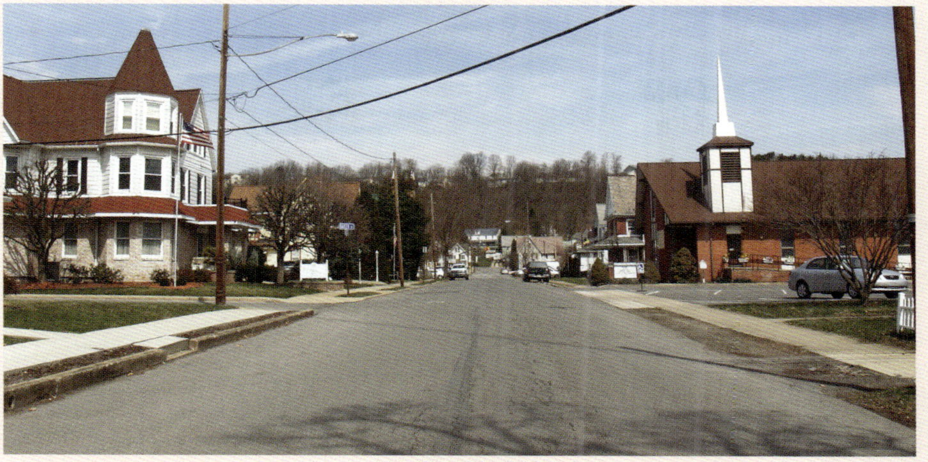

The large house on the left in these photographs of Diamond Street was the home and office of physician Dr. George Franklin Bell from 1886 until his death in 1920. He was the Lycoming County coroner from 1887 until 1893, when he became a pension examining surgeon. He was also president of the Bank of Newberry. Sanders Mortuary has occupied this site since 1946.

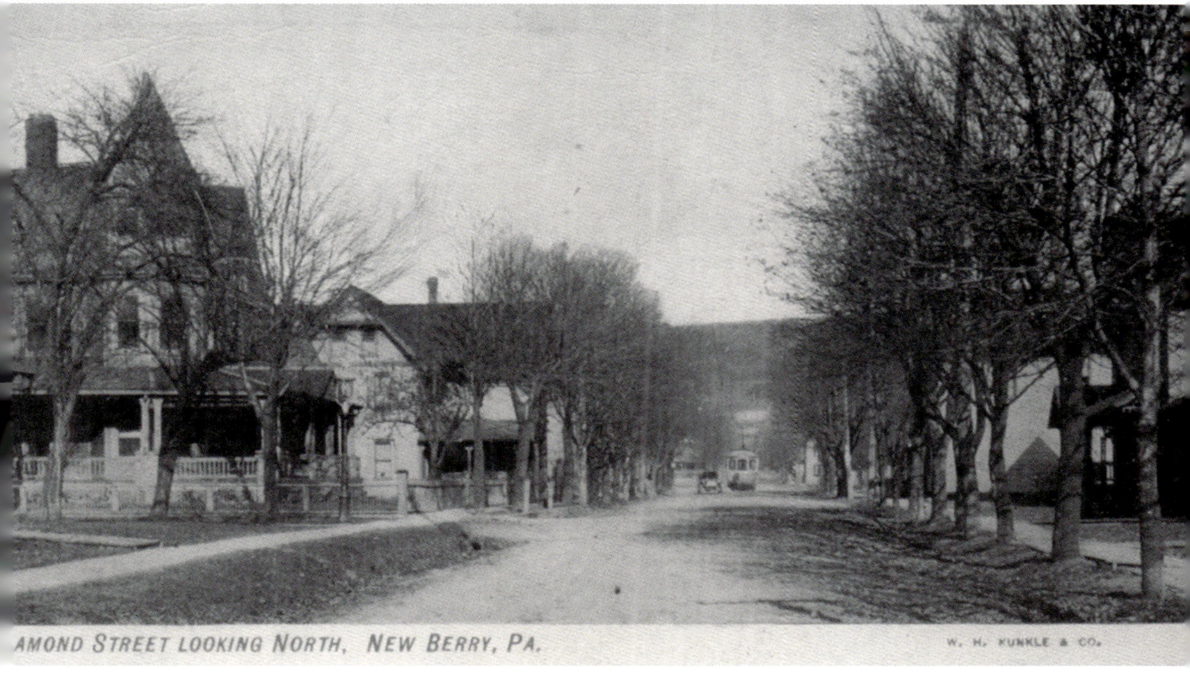